מאמר
כללי החינוך וההדרכה

THE PRINCIPLES OF
EDUCATION AND GUIDANCE

מאמר
כללי החינוך וההדרכה

THE PRINCIPLES OF
EDUCATION AND GUIDANCE

a treatise by
Rabbi Yosef Yitzchak Schneersohn
זצוקללה״ה נבג״מ זי״ע
of Lubavitch

•

translation and commentary
by
Rabbi Y. Eliezer Danzinger

New, Revised Edition

KEHOT PUBLICATION SOCIETY
770 Eastern Parkway / Brooklyn, New York 11213

THE PRINCIPLES OF
EDUCATION AND GUIDANCE

Published and Copyrighted © 1990
Revised Edition 2004
by
KEHOT PUBLICATION SOCIETY
770 Eastern Parkway / Brooklyn, New York 11213
(718) 774-4000 / Fax (718) 774-2718

Orders:
291 Kingston Avenue / Brooklyn, New York 11213
(718) 778-0226 / Fax (718) 778-4148
www.kehotonline.com

ISBN 0-8266-0457-9

Manufactured in the United States of America

CONTENTS

ב"ה

PREFACE

We hereby present *The Principles of Education and Guidance*, an instructional treatise written by the sixth Lubavitcher Rebbe, Rabbi Yosef Yitzchak Schneersohn, of blessed memory.

In 1898, at the behest of his father, Rabbi Shalom Dov-Ber, Rabbi Yosef Yitzchak began preparing a comprehensive dissertation on the topic of education. It took three months to complete. When Rabbi Yosef Yitzchak's work was finished, the magnitude of his achievement became apparent: he had constructed a formal, comprehensive treatise that illuminated virtually every aspect of the often confounding field of education.

The discourse, known as *Klalei Hachinuch Vehahadracha*, was first published in Hebrew in 1944. Nearly a half-century passed before it would see its first English rendition. In 1990, Rabbi Y. Eliezer Danzinger translated the treatise, adding numerous glosses and annotation. *The Principles of Education and Guidance*, published by Kehot Publication Society, thus became accessible to the ever broadening English-speaking audience.[1]

In the present re-edited edition, the Hebrew text has been entirely reset and vocalized, and appears with the English text on facing pages—features that are the hallmark of the acclaimed Chasidic Heritage Series. Additional annotation has been added, to make the concepts discussed in the treatise that much more accessible to the modern reader.

Two supplements have been included, both featuring stories told by Rabbi Yosef Yitzchak. The first contains captivating Chasidic stories that illustrate and develop some of

---

1. In the original English edition, the translator thanks Rabbis Uri Kaploun, Sholom B. Wineberg and Yonah Avtzon for assistance in preparing the manuscript for publication.

the themes of the treatise. The second features poignant stories from Rabbi Yosef Yitzchak's youth, where he recounts incidents that played a vital role in his education and character development.

Once again, we thank Rabbi Y. Eliezer Danzinger for devoting himself to this project, and for meticulously re-editing the manuscript and compiling the appendix. Special thanks are also due to Rabbis Ari Sollish, Avraham D. Vaisfiche and Yosef B. Friedman for their editorial assistance.

Kehot Publication Society

11 Nissan 5764

RABBI YOSEF YITZCHAK SCHNEERSOHN
זצוקללה"ה נבג"מ זי"ע
5640-5710 (1880-1950)

ונא אי ווינה י' אדר תשפ"א ל [...]
ואאווי'

כ"וב שא ה' השכב ומכונה וות איא זוה יש/י/י
בר"ן.

אתשב"ג

התב"א מכונ[...] מתירו למשה רב ז וב האנו/ וסי'פו
או תמסת ברכם ן השמי' וכן אמור [...]נ[...]זה על גיע
אסר גהן נשוו ען אנ[...] ותפן גהלית[ת] נפש' הננו הדונתיה
אסר הגעי מכונים יתענג בטה אסר פר' פינו הטבוש וסו'/
אום ן יעון אסר תפן נפסו הטהונה ותרוסה   והשת
יעוד זענ שבווטבים והר אתית פי כאנע הטבוש.
ויקי התונה ואהבה [...] העון קח לתני"ב-קמ"יש
ואוהב שוש שא הנו גוונן.

Facsimile of handwritten letter by Rabbi Yosef Yitzchak

TRANSLATOR'S INTRODUCTION

TRANSLATOR'S INTRODUCTION

"Educate the child in his way; even when
he grows old, he will not depart from it."
—Proverbs 22:6

On the 18th of Sivan 5658 (1898), Rabbi Shalom Dov-Ber Schneersohn, the fifth Lubavitcher Rebbe, charged his son, Rabbi Yosef Yitzchak (who would later succeed his father as the leader of the Chabad-Lubavitch movement), with the task of compiling a treatise on education. It was intended to serve as an educational guide for two venerable Chasidim—R. Chanoch Hendel Kugel, and R. Shmuel Gronem Esterman—who were the *mashpi'im*, spiritual mentors, in the *yeshivot* of Lubavitch and Zhembin, respectively.

The yeshivah student body was comprised initially of some twenty[1] students between the ages of eighteen and twenty. Hand picked by Rabbi Shalom DovBer himself, they were all exceptionally gifted intellectually, and were thoroughly versed in many complex Talmudic topics. Their knowledge of Chasidus, though, was scanty. And in particular, they were unfamiliar with *avodah*—divine service—as influenced and guided by the spiritual lifestyle of Chasidus.

Much has been written[2] describing the noble goals of *Tomchei Temimim*, as the yeshivah was later named by Rabbi Shalom DovBer.[3] But perhaps the yeshivah's objective can best be encapsulated by the cogent reply of the founder of Chabad-Chasidism, Rabbi Schneur Zalman of Liadi, to one who questioned him as to why he traveled all the way to Mez-

---

1. Tract on Prayer, p. 7, in the introduction. Cf. *Hatamim*, 1 p. 26, where the precise number of students is recorded as being eighteen.

2. Cf. *Maamar Kol Hayotzei L'milchemet Beit David, Sefer Hasichot 5702*, p. 141ff.

3. *Hatamim*, op. cit., pp. 25-26.

ritch to learn rather than to Vilna (which was considerably closer): "In Vilna one learns how to study Torah. In Mezritch, however, one learns how the Torah teaches himself—so that he himself becomes a Torah."[4]

Rabbi Shalom DovBer provided his son with some of his own writings on the subject of education, which he had penned ten years earlier. With these papers in hand, Rabbi Yosef Yitzchak—eighteen years old at the time—plunged into his assignment. After a few preliminary drafts, he completed his final version in just over three months, on the 21st of Elul. In his diary, Rabbi Yosef Yitzchak records his delight in completing the treatise.[5]

Many years elapsed before this treatise was first published in the year 5704 (1944), as part of a pamphlet entitled *Kuntres Chai Elul 5703*. Subsequently, it was reprinted in 5725 (1965) as an appendix to *Sefer Hasichot 5703*. The footnotes in these editions were not part of the original text, but were added by the publisher, the future Lubavitcher Rebbe, Rabbi Menachem M. Schneerson, as indicated in the preface to *Kuntres Chai Elul 5703*.

This translation includes several additional footnotes, consisting of explanatory notes and supplementary references. These footnotes appear in plain type-face, while the original footnotes from the 1944 edition appear in bold type-face. Insertions by the translator in the main body of the text have been enclosed in square brackets. Round brackets, however, have been carried forward from the original Hebrew. The chapter titles list, it should be noted, has been translated from the original text.

To facilitate the reader's comprehension of the text, transliteration of Hebrew terminology has been avoided, though the precise meaning of the original word is sometimes obscured.

For instance, two Hebrew words which have been trans-

---

4. *Likkutei Dibburim* Eng. ed., vol. 2 p. 165.

5. *Sefer Hasichot 5703*, p. 188.

lated into English throughout, and appear in the very title of this treatise—*chinuch* and *hadrachah*—have been rendered as *education* and *guidance*. Traditionally and etymologically, *chinuch* and *hadrachah* denote much more than just the transmission of knowledge. In fact, the critical distinction between teaching or instructing (*limud* and *hora'ah*), and educating or counseling, is the focus of an entire chapter (chapter two).

A translation is generally a poor substitute for the original, being perforce an adaptation and a subjective interpretation. This is true, in particular, regarding the translation of this treatise, which, despite its brevity, is replete with Chasidic concepts and terminology, is interwoven with Talmudic and Biblical phrases, and is rich in subtle and profound nuances. Yet, it is hoped that this translation will aid the reader who seeks a more profound understanding of education and guidance—a field of such paramount importance to Jewish life. And although the author addresses educators and spiritual counselors, the new vistas of insight uncovered herein will certainly prove to be of significant practical value to parents as well.

Y. Eliezer Danzinger

NOTE ON THE HEBREW TEXT: In vocalizing the Hebrew words in this edition we have followed the grammatical rules of the Holy Tongue, which occasionally differ from the traditional or colloquial pronunciation.

TRANSLATION
AND
COMMENTARY

The Principles of Education and Guidance
—comprising seventeen chapters—

1. The Doctrine of Education and Guidance.
2. Principles of Education and Guidance.
3. Man's Self-Examination and Preparation.
4. The First Provision: Self-Examination by the Educator and Counselor.
5. The Second Provision: The Preparation of the Educator and Counselor.
6. The Third Provision: Perception of a Pupil's Character and Situation.
7. The Pupil's Character.
8. Classification of People Based on Four Determinants.
9. A) Classification Based on Occupation.
10. B) Classification Based on Financial Circumstances: Poor or Rich.
11. C) Classification Based on Habit, Regardless if Good or Bad.
12. D) Classification Based on Environment and Place of Residence: A Small Town or Large City.
13. The Fourth Provision: The Educator's Understanding of the Desirable and the Repugnant, and their Limits.
14. The Fifth Provision: The Educator's Deliberate Reflection in Choosing Educational Approaches and Methods.
15. The Sixth Provision: Prioritization in Educational Approaches and Methods.
16. Intrinsic and Figurative Attributes.
17. The Seventh Provision: Praise and Reward—Rebuke and Punishment in Education and Counseling.

מַאֲמָר כְּלָלֵי הַחִנּוּךְ וְהַהַדְרָכָה
— וּבוֹ שִׁבְעָה עָשָׂר פְּרָקִים—

THE PRINCIPLES OF EDUCATION AND GUIDANCE

1.

THE FIELD OF EDUCATION AND GUIDANCE

Education and guidance constitute a comprehensive discipline with many principles concerning the proper preparation and conduct of both educator and pupil. In general, education entails tremendous responsibility, demands arduous and laborious work, and can be carried out only with profound spiritual and physical exertion.

All of man's actions—whether exceedingly difficult or simple—require a specific [revelatory] talent; for every action must evolve from its [prior] spiritual state to its [revealed] material one. The type of talent that is suitable for actualizing a particular action depends upon the type of action to be performed. And the efficacy of the resultant action is determined by the degree to which one successfully reveals this talent.

Talent is a gift from G-d. Some people are endowed by G-d with a talent for singing; others with a talent for oratory and rhetoric, or a talent for instructing; and some people are graced by G-d with a talent for educating, and so on.

Talents are [expressions of] the soul's spiritual powers—the soul's limbs. The soul's essence extends into these limbs, animating them according to their particular character, and enabling them [thereby] to carry out their unique tasks. Although the soul's essence is a [non-composite] spiritual essence that does not differentiate between the various talents [that spring from it],[1] yet talents are clearly divided by their inherent qualities and respective effects.

Talents are divided into two general groups: (a) talents that have a physical effect—such as a talent to draw and to weave, or a talent to play assorted types of musical in-

---

1. The end of ch. 6 elaborates upon this concept.

מַאֲמָר כְּלָלֵי הַחִנּוּךְ וְהַהַדְרָכָה

א.

תּוֹרַת הַחִנּוּךְ וְהַהַדְרָכָה.

הַחִנּוּךְ וְהַהַדְרָכָה הִיא תּוֹרָה שְׁלֵמָה בַּהֲלָכוֹת מְרוּבּוֹת מִסְתַּעֲפִים לְפִרְקֵי הַכְשָׁרָה וּפִרְקֵי הַנְהָגָה, הֵן מִצַּד הַמְחַנֵּךְ וְהַמַּדְרִיךְ וְהֵן מִצַּד הַמְחוּנָּךְ וְהַמּוּדְרָךְ. וּבִכְלָלוּתָהּ הִיא רַבַּת הָאַחֲרָיוּת וַעֲבוֹדָה קָשָׁה וּכְבֵדָה בִּיגִיעָה עֲצוּמָה בִּיגִיעַת נֶפֶשׁ וִיגִיעַת בָּשָׂר.

כָּל פְּעוּלּוֹת הָאָדָם אֵיזֶה שֶׁיִּהְיוּ, בֵּין הַכְּבֵדוֹת בְּיוֹתֵר וּבֵין הַקַּלּוֹת, הִנֵּה מֵאַחַר שֶׁהַפְּעוּלָּה בָּאָה מִן הָרוּחָנִי אֶל הַגַּשְׁמִי הֲרֵי הִיא דּוֹרֶשֶׁת כִּשָּׁרוֹן מְיוּחָד הַמַּתְאִים אֶל הַפְּעוּלָּה הַהִיא, וּלְפִי מַהוּת הַפְּעוּלּוֹת וְעִנְיָנָם כֵּן הֵם הַכִּשְׁרוֹנוֹת הַמַּתְאִימִים אֲלֵיהֶם, וּלְפִי אוֹפֶן הִתְגַּלּוּת כִּשְׁרוֹנוֹ כֵּן תִּהְיֶה תּוֹעֶלֶת פְּעוּלָּתוֹ.

הַכִּשָּׁרוֹן הוּא מַתְּנַת אֱלֹקִים. יֵשׁ מְחוּנָּן מֵהַשֵּׁם יִתְבָּרֵךְ בְּמַתְּנַת כִּשְׁרוֹן הַקּוֹל, בְּשִׁיר וּבְזִמְרָה, יֵשׁ מְחוּנָּן בְּכִשְׁרוֹן הַנְּאוּם וְהַהַטָּפָה, יֵשׁ מְחוּנָּן בְּכִשְׁרוֹן הַהוֹרָאָה וְיֵשׁ מְחוּנָּן בְּכִשְׁרוֹן הַחִנּוּךְ וְהַהַדְרָכָה וְכַדּוֹמֶה בִּשְׁאָרֵי הַכִּשְׁרוֹנוֹת.

אָמְנָם עִם הֱיוֹת אֲשֶׁר הַכִּשְׁרוֹנוֹת הֵם כֹּחוֹת הַנֶּפֶשׁ הָרוּחָנִית וְכוּלָּם כְּאֶחָד הֵם אֵבָרִים אֲשֶׁר עֶצֶם הַנֶּפֶשׁ מִתְפַּשֵּׁט בָּהֶם לְהַחֲיוֹתָם בְּכָל אֶחָד לְפִי עִנְיָנוֹ לָתֵת לוֹ הַכֹּחַ וְהָעוֹז לִפְעוֹל פְּעוּלָּתוֹ, וְעִם הֱיוֹת עֶצֶם הַנֶּפֶשׁ עֶצֶם רוּחָנִי הַבִּלְתִּי מְחֻלָּק בֵּין כִּשָּׁרוֹן לְכִשָּׁרוֹן, בְּכָל זֶה הֲרֵי בְּהֶכְרֵחַ שֶׁיִּתְחַלְּקוּ הַכִּשְׁרוֹנוֹת לְפִי מַהוּת מַעֲלָתָם וּלְפִי עִנְיַן פְּעוּלָּתָם.

הַהִתְחַלְּקוּת הַכְּלָלִית בְּהַכִּשְׁרוֹנוֹת הֵם לִשְׁנֵי סוּגִים: א) כִּשְׁרוֹנוֹת הַפּוֹעֲלִים בַּגֶּשֶׁם כְּמוֹ כִּשְׁרוֹן הַצִּיּוּר וּמְלֶאכֶת

struments, etc., and (b) talents that have a spiritual effect—such as a talent for oratory and rhetoric, which stir the
emotions of an audience; a talent for teaching and instructing;
or a talent for educating and counseling; and so forth.

The above division is based on [differences between] the
impact of talents outside themselves. As such, it is delineated
by the way talents are expressed within their resultant actions.
This basis of distinction between the two categories of talents
has both general and specific applications:[2] No comparison
whatsoever can be made between the way in which a talent affects the physical and the way in which it affects the spiritual.
[This is similar to the contrasts that exist among the talents
within each of these two general groups:] Just as in the realm
of related physical talents, the effects of drawing differs from
the effects of singing, so, too, do comparable distinctions exist
in the realm of related spiritual talents: the effects of educating and counselling differ from the effects of teaching and
instructing.

Synopsis

Talents are categorized by:

1) What they affect—the material or the spiritual;

2) The manner in which they are expressed within each of
the two general groups, and within the particular subgroups
of the two general groupings.

2.

PRINCIPLES OF EDUCATION AND GUIDANCE

At first glance, the field of education and guidance appears to
be quite similar to the field of teaching. Both belong to the
same spiritual talent group, since they involve the use of talents that have spiritual effects. In truth, however, they are entirely different.

---

2. In other words, the way that talents are clothed in their resultant actions differs from talent to talent. Ap-
plying this criterion in a general way,
two general groups emerge: spiritual—oriented talents and materi-

מַחֲשֶׁבֶת בְּאִימוּן יָד, אוֹ כִּשְׁרוֹן הַזִּמְרָה בְּכֵלִים שׁוֹנִים
וְכַדּוֹמֶה. ב) כִּשְׁרוֹנוֹת הַפּוֹעֲלִים בְּרוּחָנִי כְּמוֹ כִּשְׁרוֹן
הַנְּאוּם וְהַהַטָּפָה לְעוֹרֵר רִגְשׁוֹת הַשּׁוֹמְעִים, כִּשְׁרוֹן הַלִּימוּד
וְהַהוֹרָאָה, כִּשְׁרוֹן הַחִינּוּךְ וְהַהַדְרָכָה וְהַדּוֹמֶה.

אָמְנָם הִתְחַלְּקוּת זוֹ הִיא הִתְחַלְּקוּת הַסּוּגִים הַכּוֹלְלִים
מִצַּד הַשְׁפָּעָתָם מִחוּץ לָהֶם, וְהִתְחַלְּקוּת זוֹ הִיא מִצַּד
תְּפִיסַת הַכִּשְׁרוֹנוֹת בִּפְעוּלוֹתֵיהֶם וּבָאָה בְּהִתְחַלְּקוּת כְּלָלִית
וּפְרָטִית שֶׁאֵינוֹ דוֹמֶה כְּלָל תְּפִיסַת הַכִּשָּׁרוֹן בִּפְעוּלָתוֹ
בְּגֶשֶׁם לִתְפִיסָתוֹ שֶׁל הַכִּשָּׁרוֹן בִּפְעוּלָתוֹ הָרוּחָנִית, וּכְשֵׁם
שֶׁיֵּשׁ הֶבְדֵּל בְּהִתְלַבְּשׁוּתוֹ שֶׁל הַכִּשָּׁרוֹן בְּסוּג הַפּוֹעֲלִים
בְּגֶשֶׁם, דְּאֵינוֹ דוֹמֶה הִתְלַבְּשׁוּת כְּשְׁרוֹן הַצִּיּוּר בִּפְעוּלָתוֹ
לְהִתְלַבְּשׁוּתוֹ שֶׁל כְּשְׁרוֹן הַזִּמְרָה בִּפְעוּלָתוֹ, הִנֵּה כֵּן הוּא
בְּסוּג הַכִּשְׁרוֹנוֹת הַפּוֹעֲלִים בְּרוּחָנִי, דְּאֵינוֹ דוֹמֶה כְּלָל
תְּפִיסָתוֹ שֶׁל הַכִּשָּׁרוֹן בְּחִינּוּךְ וְהַדְרָכָה לִתְפִיסָתוֹ שֶׁל
הַכִּשָּׁרוֹן בְּלִימוּד וְהוֹרָאָה.

קִיצוּר. הַכִּשְׁרוֹנוֹת מִתְחַלְּקִים א) בִּפְעוּלוֹתֵיהֶם אִם
בְּגַשְׁמִי אִם בְּרוּחָנִי. ב) בִּתְפִיסָתָם בִּשְׁנֵי הַסּוּגִים וְכָל סוּג
בִּפְרָט.

ב.

כְּלָלֵי הַחִינּוּךְ וְהַהַדְרָכָה.

בְּהַשְׁקָפָה רִאשׁוֹנָה הֲרֵי תּוֹרַת הַחִינּוּךְ וְהַהַדְרָכָה
וְתוֹרַת הַהוֹרָאָה מַתְאִימוֹת הֵמָּה, לִהְיוֹת שֶׁתֵּיהֶן בְּסוּג
אֶחָד, כִּשְׁרוֹנוֹת הַפּוֹעֲלִים בְּרוּחָנִי, אֲבָל בֶּאֱמֶת שׁוֹנוֹת הֵנָּה
זוֹ מִזּוֹ בְּתַכְלִית.

---

al—oriented talents. When this criterion is applied more specifically, distinctions between talents within each group itself are discernable.

Educating and guiding is a difficult task in general. It involves harder work than does the task of a teacher instructing his students. Although teaching is also one of the hardest and most strenuous types of work, still, its difficulty is not at all comparable to the difficulty of educating and guiding. There are two reasons for this:

[First,] in teaching, an instructor is involved in [communicating] intellectual ideas:

1) Clarifying a concept, and explaining it by means of analogies and illustrations;

2) Developing a student's abilities in, a) conceiving ideas, b) comprehending the analogy and the rationale, c) with a settled and clear understanding.

In any event, the task of a teacher in his instruction is only in the area of intellect and knowledge, as even the simplest and most basic concept is still within the realm of the intellect.

This is not so in the labor of education and guidance. In most cases, the main effort of an educator lays chiefly in [transforming] base and ignoble traits [of his pupil]. This is particularly true at the beginning of a pupil's education and guidance, since "man is born [like] a wild young donkey,"[3] with animalistic impulses and behavior, drawn after what is materially good, and what is visually attractive.

[Second,] although teaching, too, carries with it great responsibility, it is not at all like the responsibility borne by an educator. An ineffective teacher at least does no harm. This is not so in the work of education and guidance—which carries enormous responsibility. If one's work in this field is not constructive, it is perforce, destructive. Therefore, the educator and mentor, both of older pupils and of younger pupils, must follow the comprehensive and indispensable prerequisites of education. Otherwise, not only will one fail to

---

3. Job 11:12.

הַחִנּוּךְ וְהַהַדְרָכָה הִיא עֲבוֹדָה קָשָׁה בִּכְלָל וַעֲבוֹדָה כְּבֵדָה יוֹתֵר מֵעֲבוֹדַת הַהוֹרָאָה שֶׁל הָרַב לְתַלְמִידָיו. עִם הֱיוֹת גַּם הַהוֹרָאָה אַחַת הָעֲבוֹדוֹת הַיּוֹתֵר קָשׁוֹת וּכְבֵדוֹת, בְּכָל זֶה אֵין הַקּוֹשִׁי כְּלָל כְּמוֹ קוֹשִׁי הָעֲבוֹדָה שֶׁל חִנּוּךְ וְהַדְרָכָה, מִפְּנֵי שְׁנֵי טְעָמִים.

בַּעֲבוֹדַת הַהוֹרָאָה הֲרֵי הִתְעַסְּקוּת הַמּוֹרֶה הִיא בְּעִנְיָנִים שִׂכְלִים:

א) לְבָאֵר אֶת הַמּוּשְׂכָּל וּלְהַסְבִּירוֹ לְהַתַּלְמִיד בִּמְשָׁלִים וְדוּגְמָאוֹת.

ב) לְפַתֵּחַ אֶת חוּשֵׁי הַתַּלְמִיד: א) בְּחָכְמַת הַהַמְצָאָה ב) בַּהֲבָנַת הַמָּשָׁל וְהַסְּבָרָא ג) בִּידִיעָה מְיֻשֶּׁבֶת וּבְרוּרָה. עַל כָּל פָּנִים עֲבוֹדָתוֹ שֶׁל הַמּוֹרֶה בְּהוֹרָאָתוֹ הִיא אַךְ וְרַק בְּעִנְיְנֵי שֵׂכֶל וּמַדָּע, כִּי גַם הַמּוּשְׂכָּל הֲכִי פָּעוּט וַהֲכִי קָטָן הִנֵּה מִסּוּג הַשֵּׂכֶל הוּא.

לֹא כֵן בַּעֲבוֹדַת הַחִנּוּךְ וְהַהַדְרָכָה, הִנֵּה, עַל הָרוֹב, הֲרֵי עִקַּר הִתְעַסְּקוּתוֹ שֶׁל הַמְחַנֵּךְ וְהַמַּדְרִיךְ הוּא בְּעִנְיְנֵי נִבּוּל וְכִיעוּר, וּבִפְרָט בְּהַתְחָלַת הַחִנּוּךְ וְהַהַדְרָכָה דְּעִיר פֶּרֶא אָדָם יִוָּלֵד בִּטְבָעִיּוֹת וּרְגִילוּת בַּהֲמִיּוֹת, לִהְיוֹת נִמְשָׁךְ אַחֲרֵי הַטּוֹב הַחוּמְרִי וְאַחֲרֵי הַנֶּחְמָד לְמַרְאֵה עֵינָיו.

עֲבוֹדַת הַהוֹרָאָה בְּלִימּוּד עִם הֱיוֹתָהּ גַּם הִיא עֲבוֹדָה רַבַּת הָאַחֲרָיוּת, אֲבָל אֵינֶנָּה כְּלָל כְּאַחֲרָיוּתָהּ שֶׁל הָעֲבוֹדָה בְּחִנּוּךְ וְהַדְרָכָה. הַהוֹרָאָה בְּלִימּוּד גַּם אִם אֵינוֹ בַּר פּוֹעַל הֲרֵי עַל כָּל פָּנִים לֹא יְקַלְקֵל, לֹא כֵן בַּעֲבוֹדַת הַחִנּוּךְ וְהַהַדְרָכָה שֶׁאַחֲרָיוּתוֹ גְּדוֹלָה מְאֹד, דְּאִם אֵינוֹ מְתַקֵּן הֲרֵי בְּהֶכְרֵחַ שֶׁיְּקַלְקֵל. וְלָכֵן הִנֵּה הַמְחַנֵּךְ וּמַדְרִיךְ אֶת מִי שֶׁהוּא, בֵּין גָּדוֹל בֵּין קָטָן בַּשָּׁנִים, בְּהֶכְרֵחַ שֶׁיִּשְׁמֹר תְּנָאִים

correct [any matter pertaining to a pupil], but one will do harm as well.

Synopsis
General prerequisites for education and guidance.

3.

MAN'S SELF-EXAMINATION AND PREPARATION
Any person desiring a life of labor[4] must set his mind and heart to examine himself in every aspect of his ethical life, as man's greatest enemy is his inborn self-love; a love that is unbridled, materialistic, dense and coarse.

Self-love is one of the evil inclination's tools. It blinds man's intelligence, dulls his heart, closes his eyes, and plugs up his ears, preventing him from perceiving his shortcomings and the mistakes caused by his sins. Because man's path, in his own eyes, is upright, his sins and transgressions—even his inherent humanity—are obscured by this self-love.

This self-love transforms a fool—devoid of discernment—into a person of stature, a dullard into a genius, an arrogant person into a humble person, an ugly[5] person into a handsome one, a cruel individual into an individual of sterling traits, an envious person into a magnanimous one, and so on.

What folly and blindness it is for the fool to mock the stupid, the dull-witted to ridicule the ignoramus, the arrogant to deride the haughty, the ugly to belittle the filthy, and likewise with regard to other moral blemishes—neglecting completely to consider their own flaws! Even when their failings are pointed out, they find hundreds of excuses and recondite reasons for every flaw and deficiency, concluding that their in-

---

4. *Avodah*, in the Hebrew. Here the meaning is divine service as it relates to the individual himself. He struggles and labors to grow spiritually by subduing his animalistic proclivities.

5. Cf. *Likkutei Sichot*, vol. 15, p. 125 ff. where the term "ugly" (*mechu'ar*) is explained in terms of being devoid of virtues.

כּוֹלְלִים וּמוּכְרָחִים, אֲשֶׁר בִּלְעָדָם הִנֵּה לֹא זוּ בִּלְבַד שֶׁלֹּא יְתַקֵּן אֶלָּא עוֹד יְקַלְקֵל.

קִיצוּר. תְּנָאִים כּוֹלְלִים בְּחִנּוּךְ וְהַדְרָכָה.

ג.

בִּקֹּרֶת הָאָדָם בְּיַחַס לְעַצְמוֹ וְהַכְשָׁרָתוֹ.

כָּל אָדָם הֶחָפֵץ בְּחַיֵּי עֲבוֹדָה צָרִיךְ לָשׂוּם דַּעְתּוֹ וְלִבּוֹ לְבַקֵּר אֶת עַצְמוֹ בְּכָל עַנְפֵי חַיָּיו הַמּוּסָרִיִּים, כִּי הַשּׂוֹנֵא הֲכִי גָדוֹל שֶׁל הָאָדָם הוּא הָ"אַהֲבַת עַצְמוֹ" הַפְרָאִית – מִצַּד הַתּוֹלָדָה שֶׁהוּא חוּמְרִי עַב וְגַס.

אַהֲבַת עַצְמוֹ הִיא אַחַת מִכְּלֵי אוּמָנָתוֹ שֶׁל הַיֵּצֶר הָרָע, הוּא הַמְעַוֵּר אֶת שֵׂכֶל הָאָדָם וּמְטַמְטֵם אֶת לִבּוֹ, סוֹתֵם אֶת עֵינָיו וְאוֹטֵם אֶת אָזְנָיו מִלְּהָבִין אֶת חֶסְרוֹנוֹתָיו וְשִׁגְיאוֹת עֲווֹנוֹתָיו, לִהְיוֹת דֶּרֶךְ אִישׁ יָשָׁר בְּעֵינָיו וְעַל כָּל פְּשָׁעָיו וַחֲטָאָיו, גַּם לְהָאֱנוֹשִׁיוּת בַּאֲשֶׁר הוּא אָדָם, תְּכַסֶּה אַהֲבָה זוֹ שֶׁהָאָדָם אוֹהֵב אֶת עַצְמוֹ.

הָ"אַהֲבַת עַצְמוֹ" עוֹשֶׂה אֶת הַשּׁוֹטֶה וְנִבְעָר מִדַּעַת לְאָדָם הַמַּעֲלָה בְּעֵינֵי עַצְמוֹ, אֶת אֲטוּם הַמּוֹחַ לְמַשְׂכִּיל, אֶת הַגֵּאֶה לְעָנָו, אֶת הַמְכוֹעָר לִיפֵה תֹאַר, אֶת הָאַכְזָר לְבַעַל מִדּוֹת יְשָׁרוֹת, אֶת הַמְקַנֵּא לְטוֹב עַיִן וְכַיּוֹצֵא בָזֶה.

כַּמָּה מִן הַשְׁטוּת וְהָעִוָּרוֹן יֵשׁ בָּזֶה, אֲשֶׁר הָאֱוִיל לוֹעֵג לְהַכְסִיל, אֲטוּם הַמּוֹחַ לַנִּבְעָר מִדַּעַת, הַגֵּאֶה לְגַס הָרוּחַ, הַמְכוֹעָר לְהַמְזוֹהָם וְכֵן בִּשְׁאָרֵי בַּעֲלֵי מוּמִין הַמּוּסָרִים מִבְּלִי הִתְחַשֵּׁב כְּלָל עִם מוּמֵי עַצְמָם. וְגַם אִם מְעוֹרְרִים אוֹתָם עַל זֶה הִנֵּה יִמְצְאוּ מֵאוֹת הִתְנַצְּלוּת וּטְעָמִים כְּמוֹסִים עַל כָּל מוּם וְחִסָּרוֹן, כִּי טָעָה הַמְעוֹרֵר לַחֲשֹׁבוֹ לְמוּם וְחִסָּרוֹן. וּמֵהֶם גַּם כְּאִלּוּ אֲשֶׁר מוּמֵיהֶם בּוֹלְטִים

formant was mistaken in thinking of it as a flaw and a fault. Among these self-deluded are some whose shortcomings are blatant and whose offenses are unbounded. Yet, these scarred individuals sin against the chosen of G-d's creatures, man, and against their very own souls, by placing themselves, with unconstrained audacity and impudence, upon a pedestal beyond the reach of self-examination.

Woe to these individuals! They betray the Divine purpose of their souls' descent from exalted heights to the nadir of depths in this world: in order to acquire fine character traits—in addition to the study of Torah and the fulfillment of its commandments. And they forfeit thereby the spiritual elevation they could have reached, and its reward in the World to Come. Moreover, they remain disgraced and forever repugnant.

The blame for all this rests completely with this inborn self-love. As an ox being led to slaughter is the man who fails to scrutinize himself. Instead [of engaging in critical introspection], he naively follows his self-love, thereby undermining—Heaven forefend—his ethical and spiritual life, and his *raison d'etre*.

Man's life in this world involves a fierce battle between good and evil, truth and falsehood, beauty and ugliness. In times of war, one of the stratagems employed is the institution of incisive and systematic inspections. Even loved ones and close friends must be watched with a keen eye—to ensure that they too are fulfilling their obligations in the campaign to vanquish the enemy. Understandably, it is crucial to monitor vigilantly and examine intensely the foe himself, especially when he disguises himself in the attire of a loved one—self-love—and deceives the person at his every step.

Therefore, the person who desires a life that is consonant with the mission that Providence has ordained for him—to illuminate the world with the light of Torah and *mitzvot*—and which nourishes him with the spiritual provisions necessary to carry out his assigned task, such a per-

וְסִרְחוֹנָם עוֹבֵר כָּל גְּבוּל, הִנֵּה בְּאַשְׁמַת אַהֲבַת עַצְמָם חוֹטְאִים בַּעֲלֵי מוּמִים הַלָּלוּ כְּלַפֵּי בְּחִיר הַנִּבְרָאִים אֲשֶׁר בָּרָא אֱלֹקִים – הוּא הָאָדָם – כְּלַפֵּי נִשְׁמָתָם לְהַרְהִיב עֹז וּלְהָעִיז לְהַעֲמִיד עַצְמָם בַּסוּג לְמַעְלָה מִן הַבִּקֹרֶת.

אוֹי וַאֲבוֹי לָהֶם לַבְּרִיּוֹת הַלָּלוּ, אֲשֶׁר לְבַד זֹאת כִּי חוֹטְאִים הֵמָּה לְאוֹתָהּ הַכַּוָּנָה אֲשֶׁר הַקָּדוֹשׁ בָּרוּךְ הוּא הוֹרִיד אֶת נִשְׁמָתָם מֵאִיגְרָא רָמָה לְבֵירָא עֲמִיקְתָּא בָּעוֹלָם זֶה לְעָבְדָהּ וּלְשָׁמְרָהּ בְּקִנְיַן הַמִּדּוֹת הַטּוֹבוֹת נוֹסָף עַל לִימּוּד הַתּוֹרָה וּשְׁמִירַת קִיּוּם הַמִּצְוֹת, וְחוּץ מִזֶּה אֲשֶׁר מְאַבְּדִים הֵם רַחֲמָנָא לִצְלָן אֶת הָעִילּוּי שֶׁהָיוּ עוֹלִים בְּמַעֲלַת הָרוּחָנִיּוּת וּבָאִים עַל שְׂכָרָם בְּעָלְמָא דְּאָתֵי, הִנֵּה עוֹד זֹאת אֲשֶׁר נִשְׁאָרִים הֵמָּה לָבוּז וּלְחֶרְפַּת עוֹלָם.

וְהָאַשְׁמָה תְּלוּיָה אַךְ וְרַק בְּהָ"אַהֲבַת עַצְמוֹ" הַתּוֹלַדְתִּית, אֲשֶׁר הָאָדָם, הַבִּלְתִּי מֵשִׂים דַּעְתּוֹ וְלִבּוֹ לְבַקֵּר אֶת עַצְמוֹ, הוֹלֵךְ אַחֲרֶיהָ בְּתֹם לֵבָב כַּשּׁוֹר לַטֶּבַח יוּבָל וּמְאַבֵּד חַס וְשָׁלוֹם אֶת חַיָּיו הַמּוּסָרִים וְהָרוּחָנִים וּמַטְּרָתוֹ הָאֱנוֹשִׁית.

חַיֵּי הָאָדָם בְּעָלְמָא דֵין הֵם מִלְחָמָה עֲצוּמָה בֵּין הַטּוֹב וְהָרַע, הָאֱמֶת וְהַשֶּׁקֶר, הַנָּאֶה וְהַמְגוּנֶּה, וּבִשְׁעַת מִלְחָמָה הִנֵּה אֶחָד הַטַּכְסִיסִים הוּא – הַבִּקֹרֶת הַחַדָּה וְהַמְסוּדֶּרֶת. אֲפִילוּ עַל אוֹהֲבִים וִידִידִים צְרִיכִים לְהַשְׁגִּיחַ בְּעַיִן פְּקִיחָא אִם מְמַלְּאִים הֵמָּה אֶת חוֹבָתָם לְהוֹעִיל לְנַצֵּחַ אֶת הָאוֹיֵב, וּמוּבָן גּוֹדֶל הֶכְרֵחַ הַהַשְׁגָּחָה הֲכִי חֲזָקָה וְהַבִּקֹרֶת הֲכִי חַדָּה עַל הָאוֹיְבִים וּבִפְרָט עַל שׂוֹנֵא הַמִּסְתַּתֵּר בְּבִגְדֵי אוֹהֵב – אַהֲבַת עַצְמוֹ – וּמַתְעֶה אֶת הָאָדָם עַל כָּל צַעַד וְצַעַד.

אֲשֶׁר עַל כֵּן הִנֵּה הָאִישׁ הֶחָפֵץ בַּחַיִּים מַתְאִימִים לְהַשְּׁלִיחוּת אֲשֶׁר גָּזְרָה עָלָיו הַהַשְׁגָּחָה הָעֶלְיוֹנָה, לְהָאִיר אֶת הָעוֹלָם בְּאוֹר תּוֹרָה וְנֵר מִצְוָה, וּמַטִּיבָה עִמּוֹ לְכַלְכְּלוֹ בְּכָל הַדָּרוּשׁ לוֹ בִּמְזוֹנוֹתָיו הָרוּחָנִים לְפִי הָעֲבוֹדָה הַמּוּטֶלֶת

son must prepare himself through critical self-examination. He must scrutinize his service [to G-d] and his conduct.

Synopsis
Self-love deceives man; self-examination prepares him for fruitful work.

4.

THE FIRST PREREQUISITE:
SELF-EXAMINATION BY THE EDUCATOR AND COUNSELOR

All people, regardless of their lineage—be they descendants of aristocracy or common folk—possess both virtues and deficiencies. G-d implanted in man's nature virtues, as they bring humanity to its perfection. And He implanted shortcomings, so that man work on his character to remove and uproot these flaws, acquiring exemplary virtues in their stead.

The labor and work that enriches the person is supreme. There is no greater pleasure than the pleasure of man's toil in transforming evil into good. The person who plows and sows a plot of choice land and produces a prosperous yield, is not as pleased as he who plows and sows poor soil and produces a prosperous yield. In addition to his monetary profit, the latter derives moral satisfaction in his handiwork and copious labor.

The reason is that working and laboring on refining one's character enriches a person with everlasting happiness. The work of replacing and exchanging evil with good, and the repulsive with the beautiful, gives a person far more pleasure than does the preoccupation with goodness and beauty—as the saying,[6] "Who among you [before coming] here, has converted darkness into light and bitterness into sweetness?"[7]

Man's nature, his virtues and shortcomings, are divisible into two categories: those that are inborn, and those formed

---

6. *Zohar* I:4b.

7. Just as G-d considers such service

to be pre-eminent (as documented here), likewise must man perforce recognize this service to be super-

עָלָיו, הִנֵּה הַהַכְשָׁרָה שֶׁיַּכְשִׁיר הָאָדָם אֶת עַצְמוֹ הוּא עַל יְדֵי הַבִּקּוֹרֶת שֶׁיְּבַקֵּר אֶת עַצְמוֹ בַּעֲבוֹדָתוֹ וּבְהַנְהָגָתוֹ.

קִצּוּר. אַהֲבַת עַצְמוֹ מַתְעָה אֶת הָאָדָם, וְהַבִּקֹּרֶת מַכְשֶׁרֶת אוֹתוֹ לַעֲבוֹדָה פּוֹרִיָּה.

ד.

תְּנַאי רִאשׁוֹן: בִּקֹּרֶת הַמְחַנֵּךְ וְהַמַּדְרִיךְ בְּיַחַס לְעַצְמוֹ.

כָּל בְּנֵי אָדָם – בְּלִי הֶבְדֵּל הַיַּחַס אִם מִגֶּזַע אֶפְרָתִים אוֹ מִגֶּזַע הַהֲמוֹנִים – בַּעֲלֵי מַעֲלָה וְחִסָּרוֹן הֵמָּה, כִּי הִטְבִּיעַ הַקָּדוֹשׁ בָּרוּךְ הוּא בְּטִבְעֵי בְּנֵי אָדָם אֶת הַמַּעֲלוֹת, בַּאֲשֶׁר הֵמָּה מִשְׁלֵימוֹת הָאֱנוֹשִׁיּוֹת, וְאֶת הַחֶסְרוֹנוֹת, בִּשְׁבִיל הָעֲבוֹדָה אֲשֶׁר הָאָדָם יַעֲבוֹד עִם עַצְמוֹ לִדְחוֹתָם לְעָקְרָם וּלְשָׁרֵשׁ אַחֲרֵיהֶם וּלְהַקְנוֹת בְּעַצְמוֹ מֵהַמַּעֲלוֹת הַנֶּאוֹתוֹת תְּמוּרָתָן.

גְּדוֹלָה עֲבוֹדָה וּמְלָאכָה הַמְעַשֶּׁרֶת אֶת בְּעָלֶיהָ, וְאֵין לְךָ נוֹעַם יוֹתֵר גָּדוֹל מֵעֲבוֹדַת הָאָדָם הַמְהַפֵּךְ אֶת הָרַע לַטּוֹב. אָדָם הַחוֹרֵשׁ וְזוֹרֵעַ בְּכִבְרַת אֶרֶץ עֲדִית וּמוֹצֵא בְּרָכָה מְרוּבָּה, הִנֵּה לֹא יִתְעַנֵּג כְּמוֹ הַחוֹרֵשׁ וְזוֹרֵעַ אַדְמַת זִבּוּרִית וּמוֹצֵא בָהּ בְּרָכָה מְרוּבָּה, כִּי בָּזֶה יִמְצָא גַם סִיפּוּק מוּסָרִי בְּפוֹעַל יָדָיו וּבַעֲבוֹדָתוֹ הַמְרוּבָּה נוֹסָף עַל הָרֶיוַח הַכַּלְכָּלִי.

וְכֵן הַדָּבָר כִּי גְּדוֹלָה עֲבוֹדָה וּמְלָאכָה מוּסָרִית הַמְאַשֶּׁרֶת אֶת בְּעָלֶיהָ בְּאוֹשֶׁר נִצְחִי, כִּי הָעֲבוֹדָה בְּחִלּוּף וּתְמוּרַת הָרַע בַּטּוֹב וְאֶת הַמְגוּנֶּה בַּנָּאֶה מְעַנֶּגֶת אֶת הָאָדָם יוֹתֵר מִשְּׁקִידַת הַטּוֹב וְהַנָּאֶה, כְּמַאֲמַר מַאן מִנְּכוֹן דִי חֲשׁוֹכָא מְהַפְּכָן לִנְהוֹרָא וְטַעֲמִין מְרִירוּ לְמִיתְקָא.

הַטְּבָעִים אֲשֶׁר בָּאָדָם, הֵן הַמַּעֲלוֹת וְהֵן הַחֶסְרוֹנוֹת, מִתְחַלְּקִים לִשְׁתֵּי פְלוּגוֹת: א) טְבָעִים תּוֹלַדְתִּיִּים, ב)

---

ior—since man is G-d's partner in the
act of creation. See *Likkutei Sichot*,

ibid., pp. 94-95, where this concept is
explained further.

by habit. From time to time, both [categories of character traits] take deeper root. Eventually inborn characteristics can become an innate and inseparable part of the person, while habits can become as [forceful as] inborn traits—as the saying, "Habit becomes nature."[8]

Understandably, the two forms of character traits—virtues and deficiencies—do not grow, extend, or take deeper root by themselves without any diligent work and effort on the person's part. "G-d has made one thing opposite the other,"[9] So just as one does not become knowledgeable or wise without prolonged study, likewise one's bad characteristics neither develop nor broaden without being continually exercised.

For this reason, we often observe children or youngsters, with terrific talent or with terrible tendencies, who come to a sudden standstill: neither their talents nor their bad dispositions develop any further. Those possessing talents retain their talents [but they grow no further], and those possessing shortcomings retain their shortcomings. The explanation for this [stagnancy] is the lack of diligence in cultivating the talents, and the scarcity of opportunities to develop of the wayward impulses.

However, even the person whose base characteristics have grown completely unrestrained, has the possibility and the capability not only to subdue and discard these traits, but to elevate them as well. He can do so by using the supernal power that G-d gives each and every Jew according to his needs—as our Rabbis have taught, "An oath is administered to him [before birth, enjoining him]: 'Be righteous....'"[10] This oath is explained as [G-d] satiating [and empowering] the soul,[11] for "according to the camel is its load."[12] That is to say, G-d bestows everyone with the spiritual powers necessary to trans-

---

8. *Shevilei Emunah, netiv* 4, *shaar* 5; Responsa of *Rama MiPano*, sec. 36; see *Yoma* 86a.

9. Ecclesiastes 7:14. Everything in one realm has its corresponding op-

posite in another realm. Hence, every aspect in the sphere of holiness has a counterpart in the sphere of the profane or evil.

10. *Niddah* 30b.

טִבְעִים רְגִילוּתָיִים. וּשְׁנֵיהֶם מִשְׁתָּרְשִׁים בָּהָאָדָם מִזְּמַן
לִזְמַן בְּעֹמֶק יוֹתֵר, עַד כִּי הַתּוֹלַדְתִּי נַעֲשֶׂה כְּמוֹ עַצְמִי
אֲשֶׁר בְּאוֹפֶן אַחֵר אִי אֶפְשָׁר, וְהָרְגִילוּתִי נַעֲשֶׂה כְּמוֹ
הַתּוֹלָדוֹתִי וּכְמַאֲמַר הֶרְגֵּל נַעֲשֶׂה טֶבַע.

מוּבָן הַדָּבָר אֲשֶׁר שְׁתֵּי הַמַּעֲרָכוֹת: א) מַעֲרֶכֶת
הַמַּעֲלוֹת, ב) מַעֲרֶכֶת הַחֶסְרוֹנוֹת – אֵינָן מִתְגַּדְלוֹת
מִתְרַחֲבוֹת וּמִשְׁתָּרְשׁוֹת מִצַּד עַצְמָם בְּלִי שׁוּם שְׁקִידַת
עֲבוֹדָה וּפוֹעַל, כִּי זֶה לְעוּמַת זֶה עָשָׂה אֱלֹקִים, וּכְמוֹ שֶׁלֹּא
יַשְׂכִּיל הָאָדָם וְיִתְחַכֵּם בְּלֹא לִימוּד הִנֵּה כֵן לֹא יִתְגַּדֵּל
וְיִתְרַחֵב הַחֶסָּרוֹן בְּלֹא שְׁקִידַת תַּשְׁמִישׁוֹ בָּהֶם.

מִטַּעַם זֶה אָנוּ רוֹאִים בְּמוּחָשׁ לְעִתִּים קְרוֹבוֹת, אֲשֶׁר
יְלָדִים אוֹ נְעָרִים בַּעֲלֵי כִּשָּׁרוֹן רַב אוֹ בַּעֲלֵי נְטִיּוֹת רָעוֹת,
הִנֵּה פִּתְאוֹם נִשְׁאָרִים עַל עָמְדָם מִבְּלִי הִתְפַּתֵּחַ, בְּבַעֲלֵי
כִּשָּׁרוֹן – כִּשְׁרוֹנוֹתֵיהֶם וּבְבַעֲלֵי נְטִיּוֹת רָעוֹת –
חֶסְרוֹנוֹתֵיהֶם. וְסִבַּת הַדָּבָר הִיא לְפִי שֶׁחָסְרָה הַשְּׁקִידָה
בְּהִתְפַּתְּחוּת הַכִּשְׁרוֹנוֹת, וַחֲסֵרוֹת הַהִזְדַּמְּנוּת בְּהִתְפַּתְּחוּת
הַנְּטִיּוֹת הָרָעוֹת.

אָמְנָם גַּם מִי שֶׁנְּטִיּוֹתָיו הָרָעוֹת, הֵן מִצַּד הַתּוֹלָדָה וְהֵן
מִצַּד הָרְגִילוּת, הִתְפַּתְּחוּ בְּאוֹפֶן פָּרוּעַ יֵשׁ לוֹ הָאֶפְשָׁרִיּוּת
וְהַיְכוֹלֶת לֹא רַק לִדְחוֹתָם וְלַהֲסִירָם מֵעָלָיו אֶלָּא גַּם
לְהַפְכָם מֵרַע לַטוֹב וּמִמְּגוּנֶּה לְנָאֶה בְּכֹחַ הָעֶלְיוֹן אֲשֶׁר נָתַן
הַקָּדוֹשׁ בָּרוּךְ הוּא בְּכָל אֶחָד וְאֶחָד מִיִּשְׂרָאֵל כְּפִי עִנְיָנָיו,
כְּמַאֲמַר רַבּוֹתֵינוּ זִכְרוֹנָם לִבְרָכָה מַשְׁבִּיעִין אוֹתוֹ תְּהִי
צַדִּיק וְכוּ' וּמְבוֹאָר וּמוּסְבָּר עִנְיַן שְׁבוּעָה זוֹ שֶׁהוּא הַשּׂוֹבַע
הַנַּפְשִׁי אֲשֶׁר לְפוּם גַּמְלָא שִׁיחֲנָא, שֶׁלְּכָל אֶחָד נוֹתֵן

---

11. See *Kuntres Uma'ayon*, discourse   12. *Ketubot* 67a.
14, ch. 1 (Eng. ed., Kehot, 1969).

form "darkness into light and bitterness into sweetness"[13]—through exerting oneself physically and spiritually in
one's [divine] service.

Synopsis

People possess virtues and shortcomings that are inborn
or acquired. One involved in the labor of self-refinement has
the ability to transform a shortcoming into a virtue.

5.

THE SECOND PREREQUISITE:
THE PREPARATION OF THE EDUCATOR AND COUNSELOR

To be fit for the position, an educator or counselor requires
special preparation—to ensure that his education or guidance
brings about the desired benefits. Not everyone who would
step forward to assume the designation of educator or counselor can accept this great responsibility, since an unsuitable
person not only fails to correct anything, but in addition
makes things worse, bearing the full blame for doing so.

The first step of an educator or counselor in preparing for
this highly responsible and holy work of education and guidance, is introspection. He must examine himself more earnestly and vigorously than a private individual. For as explained in Chapter Three, his entire moral and spiritual
existence depends on this [self-examination].

Aside from an incisive self-critique of his teaching and its
style, the educator or counselor needs to review his methodology, to ensure that it is characterized by consummate deliberation and deference. He must attempt to find sayings
that are appropriate for his lessons, and communicate them
pleasantly. In this way, the lessons will be engraved on the
heart of the pupil, appearing before the pupil's eyes even after
he leaves the presence of his educator or counselor.

The fruit of education does not grow overnight. To

---

13. *Zohar*, op. cit.

הַקָּדוֹשׁ בָּרוּךְ הוּא כֹּחוֹת רוּחָנִים לְהַפֵּךְ חֲשׁוֹכָא לִנְהוֹרָא
וְטַעֲמִין מְרִירוּ לְמִיתְקָא בַּעֲבוֹדָתוֹ בִּיגִיעַת בָּשָׂר וָנֶפֶשׁ.

קִיצוּר. בְּנֵי אָדָם הֵם בַּעֲלֵי מַעֲלוֹת וְחֶסְרוֹנוֹת
בְּתוֹלַדְתָּם וּרְגִילוּתָם. בִּיכוֹלֶת הָעוֹבֵד לַהֲפוֹךְ אֶת הַחִסָּרוֹן
לְמַעֲלָה.

ה.

תְּנַאי שֵׁנִי: הַכְשָׁרַת הַמְחַנֵּךְ וְהַמַּדְרִיךְ.

הַמְחַנֵּךְ וְהַמַּדְרִיךְ צָרִיךְ הַכְשָׁרָה מְיוּחֶדֶת לִהְיוֹת רָאוּי
לְחַנֵּךְ וּלְהַדְרִיךְ, וַאֲשֶׁר חִנוּכוֹ וְהַדְרָכָתוֹ יָבִיאוּ תּוֹעֶלֶת
נִרְצָה. לֹא כָל הַבָּא לִיטוֹל שֵׁם מְחַנֵּךְ וּמַדְרִיךְ יָכוֹל לָקַחַת
עָלָיו אַחֲרָיוּת גְּדוֹלָה כָּזוֹ, כִּי הַבִּלְתִּי מַתְאִים הִנֵּה לֹא זוֹ
בִּלְבַד שֶׁאֵינוֹ מְתַקֵּן כְּלוּם, אֶלָּא עוֹד זֹאת הוּא מְקַלְקֵל
וְהַקּוֹלָר תָּלוּי בְּצַנָּארוֹ.

רֵאשִׁית הַכְשָׁרַת הַמְחַנֵּךְ וְהַמַּדְרִיךְ לַעֲבוֹדָתוֹ רַבַּת
הָאַחֲרָיוּת וַהֲכִי קְדוֹשָׁה בְּחִנּוּךְ וְהַדְרָכָה הִיא הַבִּקּוֹרֶת.
הַמְחַנֵּךְ וְהַמַּדְרִיךְ צָרִיךְ לְבַקֵּר עַצְמוֹ, בְּיֶתֶר שְׂאֵת וְיֶתֶר עֹז
עַל אוֹתָהּ הַבִּקּוֹרֶת שֶׁאָדָם פְּרָטִי צָרִיךְ לְבַקֵּר אֶת עַצְמוֹ –
כָּאָמוּר בְּפֶרֶק ג אֲשֶׁר בָּזֶה תָּלוּי כָּל קִיּוּמוֹ הַמּוּסָרִי
וְהָרוּחָנִי.

וְהִנֵּה מִלְּבַד הַבִּקּוֹרֶת הַחַדָּה שֶׁהַמְחַנֵּךְ וְהַמַּדְרִיךְ צָרִיךְ
לְבַקֵּר אֶת עַצְמוֹ בְּהוֹרָאַת חִינּוּכוֹ וְהַדְרָכָתוֹ וְסִגְנוֹנָם,
צָרִיךְ לְבַקֵּר עַצְמוֹ בְּאוֹפַנֵּי הוֹרָאַת חִינּוּכוֹ וְהַדְרָכָתוֹ,
שֶׁיִּהְיוּ בְּתַכְלִית הַמְּתִינוּת וְהַנִּימוּס וְיִשְׁתַּדֵּל לִמְצוֹא
פִּתְגָּמִים מַתְאִימִים לְהַהוֹרָאוֹת הָהֵם וְיַבִּיעֵם בְּבִטּוּיִם יָפִים
לְמַעַן אֲשֶׁר יֵחָקְקוּ בְּלֵב הַמְּחוּנָךְ וְהַמּוּדְרָךְ וְיַעַמְדוּ לְנֶגֶד
עֵינָיו גַּם בְּעֵת יָצָא מֵאֵת פְּנֵי מְחַנְּכוֹ וּמַדְרִיכוֹ.

פְּרִי הַחִינּוּךְ וְהַהַדְרָכָה לֹא יִצְמַח בֵּין לַיְלָה וְכָל דָּבָר

reach any educational milestone with a pupil demands extraordinary effort and an appropriate amount of time. To uproot a bad disposition or habit of a pupil, or to have him acquire and become accustomed to a good character trait, demands much toil and much time—in addition to that [toil and time] which a pupil must exert himself in this regard.

An educator or counselor must realize that not only is it essential for him to use appropriate phrases in his lessons, but that their manner of expression—whether he expresses them politely and patiently, or irritably and derisively—also affects the foundation of education and guidance.

Even general displays of agitation and ridicule by an educator or counselor—for example, when an educator uses unrefined terms in referring to one of the worst of all human failings, terms that are indeed accurate [but that are nonetheless crude]—make a bad impression on a pupil. Hearing such words of scorn (although true) from the mouth of his educator, diminishes the educator's stature in the pupil's eyes.

Many educators and counselors err here. They think that seething with thunderous noise and clamor helps them achieve their goal in education or guidance. Among them are those who pummel their pupils with extremely harsh and angry language, insulting and berating them. Truly, even if the pupil becomes upset temporarily from the flaming rhetoric of the educator or counselor—his heart shrinking within him in pain, and at times, his eyes shedding bitter tears—this type of education yields no [lasting] benefit whatsoever. Any [temporary positive] effects vanish like a fleeting dream.

The benefits of true education and guidance are attainable only through the observance and meticulous[14] fulfillment of all the related prerequisites. Only then will the ed-

---

14. *B'hiddur*, in the Hebrew; lit., "with beauty." In this context, *b'hid-* *dur* means compliance beyond the minimal requirements.

וְעִנְיַן בְּחִינּוּךְ וְהַדְרָכָה, לֹא מִיבָּעֵי אֲשֶׁר לַעֲקוֹר טֶבַע אוֹ
רְגִילוּת רָעָה שֶׁל הַמְחוּנָּךְ וְהַמּוּדְרָךְ דּוֹרֵשׁ יְגִיעָה עֲצוּמָה
וּזְמַן נָכוֹן, אֶלָּא גַם לְהַקְנוֹת בּוֹ מִדָּה טוֹבָה וּלְהַרְגִּילוֹ בָּהּ
דּוֹרֵשׁ יְגִיעָה רַבָּה וּזְמַן מְרוּבֶּה, נוֹסָף עַל זֶה אֲשֶׁר
הַמְחוּנָּךְ וְהַמּוּדְרָךְ צָרִיךְ לַעֲבוֹד בְּעַצְמוֹ בָּזֶה.

הַמְחַנֵּךְ וְהַמַּדְרִיךְ צָרִיךְ לָדַעַת כִּי לֹא רַק פִּתְגָּמִים
מַתְאִימִים לְעִנְיָנֵי הוֹרָאוֹתָיו נוֹגְעִים בְּעִיקָרֵי תּוֹעֶלֶת
הַחִינּוּךְ וְהַהַדְרָכָה, אֶלָּא גַם אוֹפֶן בִּיטוּי הַפִּתְגָּמִים, אִם
בְּנִימוּס וּמְתִינוּת אוֹ בְּהִתְרַגְּשׁוּת וְזִלְזוּל, נוֹגֵעַ בִּיסוֹדֵי
תּוֹעֶלֶת הַחִינּוּךְ וְהַהַדְרָכָה.

הַהִתְרַגְּשׁוּת וְהַזִּלְזוּל אֲפִילוּ בִּכְלָל, כְּלוֹמַר שֶׁבִּשְׁעַת
שִׂיחָתוֹ שֶׁל הַמְחַנֵּךְ וְהַמַּדְרִיךְ עַל אֹדוֹת אַחַד הַחֶסְרוֹנוֹת
הֲכִי גְדוֹלִים בְּמוּמֵי בְּנֵי אָדָם קוֹרֵא אוֹתוֹ בְּשֵׁמוֹת שֶׁל
זִלְזוּל – אֲשֶׁר בֶּאֱמֶת מַתְאִימִים הֵם – הִנֵּה זֶה עוֹשֶׂה
רוֹשֶׁם רָע עַל הַמְחוּנָּךְ וְהַמּוּדְרָךְ לִשְׁמוֹעַ דִּבְרֵי זִלְזוּל –
אֲפִילוּ אֲמִיתִּים – מִפִּי מְחַנְּכוֹ וּמַדְרִיכוֹ וּמִתְמַעֵט עֶרְכּוֹ שֶׁל
הַמְחַנֵּךְ וְהַמַּדְרִיךְ בְּעֵינֵי הַמְחוּנָּךְ וְהַמּוּדְרָךְ.

רַבִּים מֵהַמְחַנְּכִים וְהַמַּדְרִיכִים טוֹעִים בָּזֶה מַה
שֶּׁחוֹשְׁבִים אֲשֶׁר בְּהִתְרַגְּשׁוּת בְּקוֹל רַעַם וָרַעַשׁ יַגִּיעוּ
לְמַטְרָתָם בְּחִינּוּךְ וְהַדְרָכָה, וּמֵהֶם מִתְנַפְּלִים עַל הַמְחוּנָּךְ
וְהַמּוּדְרָךְ בְּדִבְרֵי רוֹגֶז בִּדְבָרִים קָשִׁים כְּגִידִים וִיחָרְפֵנוּ
וִיגַדְּפֶנוּ, וּבֶאֱמֶת הִנֵּה גַם אִם לְשָׁעָה מִתְרַגֵּשׁ הַמְחוּנָּךְ
וְהַמּוּדְרָךְ מִלַּפִּידֵי אֵשׁ אִמְרֵי פִּי הַמְחַנֵּךְ וְהַמַּדְרִיךְ וּלְבָבוֹ
מִתְכַּוֵּוץ מִצַּעַר וְלִפְעָמִים הִנֵּה גַם יִבְכֶּה בְּמַר נַפְשׁוֹ,
הִנֵּה חִינּוּךְ וְהַדְרָכָה זוֹ לֹא יָבִיאוּ שׁוּם תּוֹעֶלֶת וְכַחֲלוֹם
יָעוּף.

תּוֹעֶלֶת הַחִינּוּךְ וְהַהַדְרָכָה הָאֲמִיתִּית הוּא רַק בִּשְׁמִירַת
כָּל הַתְּנָאִים הָאֲמוּרִים בָּזֶה וּבְמִילּוּאָן בְּהִידּוּר וְאָז יִהְיֶה

ucation and guidance endure forever, and manifold blessings
will be bestowed upon the educator or counselor.

Synopsis

Only when accompanied by composure, courtesy, and
pleasant speech—using apt expressions—will education and
guidance be purposeful.

6.

THE THIRD PREREQUISITE:

AWARENESS OF A PUPIL'S CHARACTER AND SITUATION

The pupil's character[15] and his situation[16] are the two central
pillars upon which the entire length and breadth of education
and guidance rests. For education and guidance begin by
purging the [pupil's] filth [that soils his good characteristics]
and by removing [his] coarse failings. Thus, the educator and
counselor must pay particular attention, in an organized manner, to accurately appraise a pupil's character.[17]

This evaluation [of a pupil by an educator or counselor] is
more strenuous and taxing than the [comparable] appraisal of
a student by his teacher.

In order for a teacher to ground his student in the understanding and comprehension of concepts, he must gauge the
student's abilities in, and natural aptitude for, creative cogni-
tion, explanatory perception, and settled and mellow reflection. After doing so, a teacher can frame the concept in a
way that the student will be able to grasp it, choosing the [ap-
propriate] methods and approaches to communicate this concept. Through such systematic instruction, a teacher will suc-

---

15. MAHUT, in the Hebrew. Lit.,
"what it is," from the two Hebrew
words, "*mah hu.*" Often translated as
"the essence and the inner nature."

16. The pupil's "situation" refers to
conditions explained in chapters 8 to
11.

17. "Just as wearing *tefillin* everyday
is a mitzvah commanded by the Torah to every individual, regardless of
his standing in Torah, whether deeply
learned or simple, likewise is it an absolute duty for every person to spend
a half hour every day thinking about
the education of his children, and to

דְּבַר הַחִנּוּךְ וְהַהַדְרָכָה בְּקִיּוּם נִצְחִי וּבְרָכוֹת מַאֲלִיפוֹת יָחוּלוּ עַל רֹאשׁ הַמְחַנֵּךְ וְהַמַּדְרִיךְ.

קִיצוּר. תּוֹעֶלֶת הַחִנּוּךְ וְהַהַדְרָכָה הִיא רַק כְּשֶׁבָּא בִּמְתִינוּת נִימוּס וְיוֹפִי הַבִּיטוּי בְּפִתְגָּמִים מַתְאִימִים.

ו.

תְּנַאי שְׁלִישִׁי: הַכָּרַת הַמְחַנֵּךְ וְהַמַּדְרִיךְ בְּמַהוּת הַמְחוּנָּךְ וְהַמּוּדְרָךְ וּמַצָּבוֹ.

מַהוּתוֹ וּמַצָּבוֹ שֶׁל הַמְחוּנָּךְ וְהַמּוּדְרָךְ הֵם שְׁנֵי עַמּוּדֵי הַתָּוֶךְ, אֲשֶׁר עִנְיָן הַחִנּוּךְ וְהַהַדְרָכָה בְּכָל הֶקֵּפוֹ וְרָחְבּוֹ נִשְׁעָן עֲלֵיהֶם, לִהְיוֹת כִּי הַתְחָלַת הַחִנּוּךְ וְהַהַדְרָכָה הִיא בִּדְחִיַּת הַזִּיהוּם וַהֲסָרַת הָרַע הַגַּס אִם כֵּן אֵיפוֹא עַל הַמְחַנֵּךְ וְהַמַּדְרִיךְ לְיַיחֵד שִׂימַת לֵב מְסוּדֶּרֶת לִמְדוֹד הֵיטֵב מַהוּת הַמְחוּנָּךְ וְהַמּוּדְרָךְ.

מְדִידָה זוֹ הִיא עֲבוֹדָה קָשָׁה וּכְבֵדָה יוֹתֵר מִמְּדִידָתוֹ שֶׁל הַמּוֹרֶה הַמּוֹדֵד מַהוּת תַּלְמִידוֹ.

הָרַב הָעוֹסֵק בַּהוֹרָאָה וְחָפֵץ לְהַעֲמִיד אֶת תַּלְמִידוֹ עַל בְּסִיס יְדִיעָה וַהֲבָנָה בְּמוּשְׂכָּלוֹת הִנֵּה בְּהֶכְרַח שֶׁיִּמְדּוֹד מַהוּת כִּשְׁרוֹנוֹת הַתַּלְמִיד וְחוּשָׁיו א) בְּהַמְצָאָה. ב) בְּהַסְבָּרָה. ג) בְּהִתְיַישְׁבוּת, וְאָז יוּכַל הַמּוֹרֶה לְצַיֵּיר בְּעַצְמוֹ אוֹתוֹ הַמּוּשְׂכָּל שֶׁיּוּכַל הַתַּלְמִיד לְקַבְּלוֹ, וּבוֹחֵר בְּאוֹפַנֵּי וְדַרְכֵי הַהוֹרָאָה וְאָז יַצְלִיחַ בְּהוֹרָאוֹתָיו, אֲשֶׁר לֹא זוֹ בִּלְבַד אֲשֶׁר הַתַּלְמִיד יֵדַע דְּבַר הַלִּימּוּד עַל בּוּרְיוֹ, אֶלָּא עוֹד זֹאת

---

do everything in his power–and beyond his power–to inspire them to follow the path along which they are being guided." (*Hayom Yom*, 22 *Tevet*)

ceed, not only in assuring the student's clear understanding of the material, but also in developing the student's abilities and aptitude.

An assessment of a pupil's essential character, however, is entirely different. It consists mainly in measuring: the degree of uncleanliness of bad traits, the extent of the predominance of matter over form[18] and the depth of its entrenchment. In this way, an educator or counselor can perceive the essential character of a pupil.

Yet, this analysis still does not suffice. A pupil's *situation* must also be considered closely, since his situation and surroundings[19] are pivotal to his education and guidance.

Only through the insight gleaned by assessing the [pupil's] essential character, and by considering the [pupil's] situation, can educators and counselors aspire to obtain positive results.

Common sense tells us that all people are equal in their possession of body and soul. Moreover, it cannot possibly be said that the soul's essence has virtues or deficiencies—to maintain that the essence of one soul is inherently virtuous and that the essence of another soul is innately blemished. This is patently not so. All souls in their quintessence are whole and complete. They differ from one another only in the areas and the ways in which their soul-powers manifest themselves. In this [context], distinctions of essential character traits do exist among people, whether they are children or adults.

Synopsis

Souls are all equal.[20] The differences in people's character are attributable to [differences in] the manifestation of their soul-faculties.

---

18. "Matter" *(chomer)* refers to the material aspect of a being; "form" *(tzurah)* refers to its spiritual aspect.

See *Hayom Yom, 7 Kislev.*

19. The subject of chapter 12.

אֲשֶׁר בְּהוֹרָאָה מְסוּדֶּרֶת הַלֵּזוּ הֲרֵי הָרַב מְפַתֵּחַ כִּשְׁרוֹנוֹת הַתַּלְמִיד וְחוּשָׁיו.

אָמְנָם הַמְּדִידָה בְּמַהוּת הַמְּחוּנָךְ וְהַמּוּדְרָךְ הִיא בְּאוֹפֶן אַחֵר לְגַמְרֵי, לִהְיוֹתָהּ בְּעִיקָרָה מְדִידַת גּוֹדֶל הַזִּיהוּם בְּמִדּוֹת רָעוֹת וּבְהִתְגַּבְּרַת הַחוֹמֶר עַל הַצּוּרָה וְעוֹמֶק הַשְּׁרָשָׁתָהּ, וְאָז יוּכַל הַמְּחַנֵּךְ וְהַמַּדְרִיךְ לְהַכִּיר מַהוּתוֹ שֶׁל הַמְּחוּנָךְ וְהַמּוּדְרָךְ.

וְהִנֵּה מְדִידָה זוֹ אֵינָהּ מַסְפֶּקֶת עֲדַיִין, וְצָרִיךְ לְהִתְעַנְיֵין גַּם בְּמַצָּבוֹ שֶׁל הַמְּחוּנָךְ וְהַמּוּדְרָךְ, לִהְיוֹת כִּי הַמַּצָּב וְהַסְּבִיבָה הֵם יְסוֹדוֹת עִקָּרִיִּים בְּחִינּוּךְ וְהַדְרָכָה.

וְרַק בְּהַכָּרַת שְׁנֵי עִנְיָנִים אֵלּוּ: א) מְדִידַת הַמַּהוּת ב) הִתְעַנְיְנוּת בְּמַצָּב – יָכוֹל הַמְּחַנֵּךְ וְהַמַּדְרִיךְ לְקַוּוֹת לְתוֹצָאוֹת טוֹבוֹת.

הַשֵּׂכֶל הַבָּרִיא מַרְאֶה לָדַעַת, אֲשֶׁר כָּל בְּנֵי אָדָם מִשְׁתַּוִּים הֵמָּה כְּאֶחָד שֶׁהֵם בַּעֲלֵי גוּף וָנֶפֶשׁ, וְעוֹד יוֹתֵר אֲשֶׁר אִי אֶפְשָׁר לוֹמַר שֶׁיֵּשׁ עִילּוּיִם וּמַחְסוֹרִים בְּעֶצֶם הַנֶּפֶשׁ עַצְמוֹ, שֶׁנֹּאמַר שֶׁעֶצֶם הַנֶּפֶשׁ הַזֹּאת הוּא בַּעַל מַעֲלָה וְעֶצֶם הַנֶּפֶשׁ הַזֹּאת הוּא בַּעַל חִסָּרוֹן וְאֵין הָעִנְיָן כֵּן, אֶלָּא הַנְּפָשׁוֹת כּוּלָּן בְּעֶצֶם מַהוּתָן שְׁלֵימוֹת הֵנָּה עַל צַד שְׁלֵימוּת הַנֶּפֶשׁ, וּמַה שֶּׁיֵּשׁ לְחַלֵּק בְּעִנְיַן הַנְּפָשׁוֹת הוּא רַק בְּעִנְיְנֵי וְאוֹפַנֵּי הִתְגַּלּוּת כּוֹחוֹתֵיהֶן וּבָזֶה הוּא הִתְחַלְּקוּת מַהוּתֵי בְּנֵי אָדָם בֵּין קְטַנִּים וּבֵין גְּדוֹלִים.

קִיצוּר. הַנְּפָשׁוֹת מַתְאִימוֹת וְהִתְחַלְּקוּת מַהוּתָם תְּלוּיָה בְּהִתְגַּלּוּת כּוֹחוֹתֵיהֶם.

---

20. *Tanya*, ch. 32; see *Lessons in Tanya*, vol. 1, p. 422, fn. 2.

7.

Matters of education and guidance are relevant not only to children, but to all people, regardless of their age. Although applied differently to children and adults, the essential aspects of education and guidance pertain equally to both.

An educator or counselor must assess a pupil's character in order to ascertain the pupil's inborn abilities and natural virtues. The pupil's deficiencies and conduct must also be carefully weighed. Only then can an educator organize the overall educational process—especially if he must correct some specific fault—since everything depends upon the essential character.

Some actions, when performed by a particular person, are considered seriously flawed—and the perpetrator degrades himself and others thereby. But when someone else—of lesser abilities, of smaller stature, or of a different nature—performs these very same actions, they do not reflect poorly on him. For example, if a person of prominence, renowned for his noble virtues, is not careful in refraining from prattling and the like, then this is tantamount to a desecration of G-d's name; as the Talmud relates in several places,[21] "A distinguished person is different." This is not the case with a simple fellow. Likewise, if a man is excessively preoccupied with his appearance, primping himself with fine, stylish clothing, and grooming his hair, this is a serious fault; for a woman, this behavior is quite acceptable.[22]

An educator may [mistakenly] aspire to elevate a simple pupil to the level of one who inherently possesses outstanding abilities and character, by stripping the pupil of every speck of impurity, and by inculcating within him the sterling virtues of a high-minded person. However, not only

---

21. E.g., *Brachot* 19a, *Shabbat* 51a, *Megillah* 22b. This expression is actually found no less than fourteen times in the Talmud.

22. Lit. "an adornment"; cf. *Ketubot* 59b.

ז.

מַהוּת הַמְחוּנָךְ וְהַמּוּדְרָךְ.

עִנְיַן הַחִנּוּךְ וְהַהַדְרָכָה אֵינוֹ מְיוּחָד דַּוְקָא לִקְטַנִּים כִּי
אִם הוּא כְּלָלִי מִבְּלִי הֶבְדֵּל שָׁנִים, וְרַק זֶה שֶׁמִּשְׁתַּנֶּה
וּמִתְחַלֵּף לְפִי הַשָּׁנִים, הַכַּוָּנָה שֶׁהַחִנּוּךְ וְהַהַדְרָכָה מִשְׁתַּנֶּה
בֵּין קְטַנִּים לִגְדוֹלִים רַק בְּהַמְצִיאוּת דְּהַחִנּוּךְ וְהַהַדְרָכָה, אֲבָל
בְּמַהוּת עִנְיַן הַחִנּוּךְ וְהַהַדְרָכָה אֵין הֶבְדֵּל כְּלָל אִם הוּא
בִּשְׁבִיל קְטַנִּים אוֹ בִּשְׁבִיל גְּדוֹלִים.

הַמְחַנֵּךְ וְהַמַּדְרִיךְ צָרִיךְ לִמְדוֹד אֶת מַהוּתוֹ שֶׁל הַמְחוּנָךְ
וְהַמּוּדְרָךְ וְכַוָּנַת מְדִידָה זוֹ הַיְנוּ לָדַעַת אֶת כִּשְׁרוֹנוֹתָיו
וּמַעֲלוֹתָיו הַטִּבְעִיִּים, וְכֵן לִשְׁקוֹל בַּפֶּלֶס אֶת חֶסְרוֹנוֹתָיו וְאֶת
דַּרְכֵי הַנְהָגָתוֹ, אֲשֶׁר רַק אָז יָכוֹל לְסַדֵּר אוֹפֶן הַחִנּוּךְ
בִּכְלָל וּבִפְרָט אִם נִדְרָשׁ לְתַקֵּן אֵיזֶה חִסָּרוֹן פְּרָטִי, לִהְיוֹת
כִּי הַכֹּל תָּלוּי לְפִי הַמַּהוּת.

יֵשׁ לְךָ דָבָר אֲשֶׁר אִם אִישׁ זֶה עוֹשֶׂה זֹאת לְעַוֵּל יֵחָשֵׁב
לוֹ וּמְגַנֶּה עַצְמוֹ וַאֲחֵרִים, מַה שֶּׁאֵין כֵּן אִם אַחֵר הוּא
הָעוֹשֶׂה דָבָר זֶה עַצְמוֹ, הֵן שֶׁהוּא נָמוּךְ מֵהָרִאשׁוֹן
בְּמַעֲלוֹתָיו וְכִשְׁרוֹנוֹתָיו וְהֵן שֶׁהוּא מַהוּת אַחֵר בִּכְלָל. עַל
דֶּרֶךְ מָשָׁל אָדָם הַגָּדוֹל הַמְפוֹרְסָם בְּמַעֲלוֹתָיו אִם לֹא
יִשְׁמוֹר מִלְּדַבֵּר שִׂיחָה בְּטֵלָה וְכַדוֹמֶה לְחִלּוּל הַשֵּׁם יֵחָשֵׁב,
וְלֹא כֵן אִישׁ הַפָּשׁוּט. וּכְמוֹ שֶׁמָּצִינוּ בַּגְּמָרָא בְּכַמָּה מְקוֹמוֹת
אָדָם חָשׁוּב שָׁאֲנִי. וְכֵן אִם הָאִישׁ יִתֵּן נַפְשׁוֹ וְדַעְתּוֹ עַל
עִנְיְנֵי הַקִּשּׁוּט בִּבְגָדִים נָאִים וְיָפִים וּלְסַלְסֵל בִּשְׂעָרוֹ
וְכַדוֹמֶה לְעַוֵּל גָּדוֹל יֵחָשֵׁב – וְהָאִשָּׁה תַּכְשִׁיט הוּא לָהּ.

הַמְחַנֵּךְ וְהַמַּדְרִיךְ אִם יַעֲלֶה בְדַעְתּוֹ לְהַעֲלוֹת אֶת
הָאָדָם הַפָּשׁוּט לְרוּם הַמַּעֲלוֹת שֶׁל אָדָם גָּדוֹל בַּעַל
כִּשְׁרוֹנוֹת מוּפְלָגִים וּבַעַל מֶזֶג טוֹב מוּפְלָא, עַל יְדֵי שֶׁיָּסִיר
הַפְּסוֹלֶת וְהַסִּיגִים הַיּוֹתֵר דַּקִּים אֲשֶׁר בְּמִדּוֹתָיו וְיִפְעוֹל

will the educator fail to affect a correction or improvement beyond that which the simple fellow is capable of reaching, but quite the contrary: By desiring to uplift the pupil above his capacity to the station of an outstanding intellectual and an individual of exceptionally refined character traits, the educator will ruin him—he will cause him to veer from the [proper] path.

In the book *Duties of the Heart*,[23] in the section entitled "The Gate of Introspection," chapter two, the author ponders and questions whether the standard of self-critique is the same for all people. He concludes, "People's pursuit of achievement in Torah, and of matters relating to their [portion in the] world (i.e. the World to Come), vary in accordance with each person's perception, intelligence and clarity of understanding. Each person is obligated to ponder what is his duty in the service of the Creator, exalted be He, in accordance with his recognition of the Creator's general and particular beneficences."

It is self-understood that every person is obligated to learn to the extent of his abilities, by studying alone or by learning from lecturers at public classes. One is enjoined to exert oneself to know the goodness of the Creator, i.e., Providence. Namely, that G-d watches over all creatures, providing them with life, as the verse indicates, "You open up Your hand and satisfy the desire of every living thing."[24] One must also realize and acknowledge, in particular, the providence extended to him and his family. Yet, the foregoing is obligatory only in proportion to the quality of one's essential nature.

This is axiomatic and requires no proof: a person's divine service must be commensurate with his nature and ca-

---

23. *Chovot Halevavot* is a classic theological work on the Jewish principles of faith and man's inner relationship to himself and to G-d, by Rabbenu Ba-

chya ben Yosef Ibn Pakudah, *Dayan* of Saragosa, Spain (c. 12th century). Written originally in Arabic, it was later translated into Hebrew by the fa-

עָלָיו שֶׁיִּהְיוּ בּוֹ מַעֲלוֹת הָאָדָם הַמְעוּלָה, הִנֵּה לֹא זוֹ בִּלְבָד
שֶׁלֹּא יִפְעוֹל בּוֹ שׁוּם דְּבַר תִּיקּוּן וְעִילּוּי יוֹתֵר מֵהָרָאוּי
לוֹ, אֶלָּא אַדְּרַבָּא בָּזֶה שֶׁרוֹצֶה לְהַגְבִּיהוּ מִמַּהוּתוֹ הָעַצְמִי
לְרוּם מַעֲלַת חָכָם מוּפְלָג וּבַעַל מֶזֶג בְּמִדּוֹת תְּרוּמִיּוֹת הִנֵּה
הוּא מְקַלְקֵל אוֹתוֹ, עֶר וֶועט אִים אַרַאפְּשְׁלָאגֶן פוּן
וֶועג.

בְּסֵפֶר חוֹבוֹת הַלְּבָבוֹת שַׁעַר חֶשְׁבּוֹן הַנֶּפֶשׁ פֶּרֶק ב׳:
(חוֹקֵר וְשׁוֹאֵל) אִם חֶשְׁבּוֹן כָּל בְּנֵי אָדָם שָׁוֶה אִם לֹא,
נֶאֱמַר (בָּא לִידֵי מַסְקָנָא) כִּי הַתְּשׁוּבָה בָּזֶה שֶׁהִשְׁתַּדְּלוּת
בְּנֵי אָדָם בְּעִנְיְנֵי תּוֹרָתָם וְעוֹלָמָם (רוֹצֶה לוֹמַר עוֹלָם הַבָּא)
יִתְחַלֵּף כְּפִי הִתְחַלְּפוּת הַכָּרָתָם וְשִׂכְלָם וְזִכוּת הֲבָנָתָם, וְכָל
אֶחָד וְאֶחָד מֵהֶם מְצֻוֶּה לַחְשׁוֹב עִם נַפְשׁוֹ בְּמַה שֶׁהוּא
חַיָּיב בּוֹ מֵעֲבוֹדַת הַבּוֹרֵא יִתְבָּרֵךְ כְּפִי הַכָּרָתוֹ בְּטוֹבוֹת
הַבּוֹרֵא הַכּוֹלְלוֹת וְהַמְיוּחָדוֹת.

הַדָּבָר מוּבָן מֵאֵלָיו אֲשֶׁר כָּל אָדָם מְחוּיָּיב לִלְמוֹד כָּל
מַה שֶׁאֶפְשָׁר לוֹ לְהָבִין לִלְמוֹד בְּעַצְמוֹ אוֹ לִשְׁמוֹעַ מִפִּי
אֲחֵרִים מַגִּידֵי שִׁעוּרִים בָּרַבִּים וּלְהִשְׁתַּדֵּל שֶׁיֵּדַע טוֹבַת
הַבּוֹרֵא, הַיְינוּ הַהַשְׁגָּחָה פְּרָטִית שֶׁהוּא יִתְבָּרֵךְ מַשְׁגִּיחַ
וּמְחַיֶּה אֶת כְּלָלוּת הַנִּבְרָאִים כָּאָמוּר פּוֹתֵחַ אֶת יָדֶיךָ
וּמַשְׂבִּיעַ לְכָל חַי רָצוֹן וְלָשׁוּם מוֹחוֹ וְדַעְתּוֹ עַל הַהַשְׁגָּחָה
הַפְּרָטִית מֵאִתּוֹ יִתְבָּרֵךְ עָלָיו וְעַל בְּנֵי בֵיתוֹ בִּפְרָט, בְּכָל זֶה
חִיּוּב זֶה הוּא רַק לְפִי מַעֲלַת מַהוּתוֹ.

וְזֶה דָּבָר מוּסְכָּם אֵינוֹ צָרִיךְ לִרְאָיוֹת, וְכַמַּאֲמָר הַרְבֵּה
עָשׂוּ כְּרַבִּי שִׁמְעוֹן בֶּן יוֹחַאי וְלֹא עָלְתָה בְּיָדָם, כִּי כָּל אֶחָד

---

mous translator, Rabbi Yehudah Ibn   24. Psalms 145:16.
Tibbon (approx. in the year 1180).

pabilities, as the saying,[25] "Many attempted to emulate the ways of Rabbi Shimon bar Yochai, and were unsuccessful."[26]

Synopsis

The ideal education or guidance is possible only when tailored to a pupil's character.

8.

CLASSIFICATION OF PEOPLE BASED ON FOUR DETERMINANTS

People vary in four ways:

1) Their general occupation: full-time Torah scholars[27] or business people;
2) Their financial situation: wealthy or poor;
3) Their habits: whether good or bad;
4) Their place of residence: in a small or large city.

Now although all six types[28] of people—1) Torah scholars, 2) businessmen, 3) rich people, 4) paupers, 5) inhabitants of small cities, 6) and inhabitants of large cities—are all obligated to observe the Torah's commandments, to establish fixed times for Torah study, and to conduct themselves uprightly, yet they are distinct insofar as their education and guidance relates to their day-to-day affairs.

To be well-structured and secure, education and guidance must be tailored to a pupil's age.[29]

"Man is born [like] a wild young donkey,"[30] and as explained in *Midrash Rabbah, Kohelet,* chapter one, the pro-

---

25. *Brachot* 35b.

26. Also *Yalkut Shimoni Devarim*, ch. 11, *remez* 863. Rabbi Shimon opined that a worthy person could study Torah all day, and "his work would be performed for him by others." Many who were not sufficiently meritorious followed his principle only to find that the anticipated profits did not materialize.

27. *Yoshvei ohel,* in the Hebrew, lit., "dwellers in the tent (of Torah)."

28. In stating that there are six types of people, Rabbi Yosef Yitzchak excludes from consideration a person's habits ("whether good or bad"), the third way in which people differ. Possibly, since a person's habits are not readily identifiable, and a single person may have both positive and neg-

וְאֶחָד צָרִיךְ לִהְיוֹת דַּרְכֵי עֲבוֹדָתוֹ לְפִי מַהוּתוֹ וְכִשְׁרוֹנוֹתָיו.

קִיצוּר. הַחִינּוּךְ וְהַהַדְרָכָה הַמְעוּלָּה הוּא רַק כְּשֶׁהוּא לְפִי מַהוּת הַמְחוּנָּךְ וְהַמּוּדְרָךְ.

ח.

הִתְחַלְּקוּת בְּנֵי אָדָם מִצַּד אַרְבָּעָה עִנְיָנִים.

בְּנֵי אָדָם מִתְחַלְּקִים עַל פִּי אַרְבָּעָה עִנְיָנִים: א) לְפִי כְּלָלוּת עִסְקָם: יוֹשְׁבֵי אֹהֶל אוֹ בַּעֲלֵי עֲסָקִים. ב) לְפִי מַצָּבָם: עֲשִׁירִים אוֹ עֲנִיִּים. ג) לְפִי רְגִילוּתָם בְּלִי הֶבְדֵּל אִם טוֹב אוֹ רָע. ד) לְפִי מְקוֹם מוֹשָׁבָם: בְּעִיר קְטַנָּה אוֹ גְדוֹלָה.

שֵׁשׁ מִפְלָגוֹת בְּנֵי אָדָם: א) יוֹשְׁבֵי אֹהֶל. ב) בַּעֲלֵי עֲסָקִים. ג) עֲשִׁירִים. ד) עֲנִיִּים. ה) דָּרִים בְּעִיר קְטַנָּה. ו) דָּרִים בְּעִיר גְדוֹלָה, עִם הֱיוֹת אֲשֶׁר כֻּלָּם כְּאֶחָד מְחוּיָּבִים בִּשְׁמִירַת קִיּוּם הַמִּצְוֹת מַעֲשִׂיּוֹת וּקְבִיעוּת עִתִּים לַתּוֹרָה וְהַנְהָגָה בְּמִדּוֹת יְשָׁרוֹת, בְּכָל זֶה הִנֵּה הֵם מִתְחַלְּקִים בְּעִנְיְנֵי חִינּוּךְ וְהַדְרָכָה כָּל מִפְלָגָה וּמִפְלָגָה לְפִי אוֹרְחָה בַּחַיִּים הַיּוֹם יוֹמִיִּים.

הַחִינּוּךְ וְהַהַדְרָכָה הַמְסוּדֶּרֶת וְהַבְּטוּחָה צְרִיכָה לְהַתְאִים לְגִיל הַמְחוּנָּךְ וְהַמּוּדְרָךְ.

עִיר פֶּרֶא אָדָם יִוָּלֵד, וּכְמְבוֹאָר בְּמִדְרָשׁ רַבָּה קֹהֶלֶת

---

ative habits, we can't then say that there are two additional types of people: one type with good habits, and another with bad ones.

29. Now Rabbi Yosef Yitzchak qualifies the import of the above classifications of people. When educating children, the aforementioned distinctions are largely inapplicable. When educating grownups, however, their age is no longer a major factor in the equation—only their general type classes, which by adulthood have already emerged.

30. Job 11:12.

gression of man's growth is as follows: "At one year old, a child is like a king; ... at two and three years old, similar to a pig; ... at ten years old, he jumps like a kid goat," and so forth.[31]

A young child's education and guidance differs from an older child's. A young child's education is primarily in cleanliness, modesty and proper manners, that he not eat like a glutton, and in other similar small, yet essential matters, for these constitute the main differences between an animal and a human being. An older child's education and guidance is on a higher level. His education is chiefly [in the following areas]: to observe the recitation of *birchot hanehenin*,[32] [to cultivate a proper attitude toward] study, [to develop] respect for others, to honor one's parents and to obey one's teachers. Education of a child at this age is different from the education of one who is approaching the age of *bar mitzvah,* when the emphasis is placed on fulfilling the commandments meticulously, observing the times of communal prayer, studying diligently, being careful not to waste time, and learning from those superior to him. Thus, education characteristically elevates a pupil from level to level, until he reaches the level that best suits him.

Ethical sustenance is similar to bodily sustenance: Everyone knows that good meat and strong broth strengthen man's faculties more than does a drop of milk in sweetened water. Nevertheless, if one were to feed strong soup and good meat to a one-month-old baby, the infant would die. And if one were to feed only sweetened water with a drop of milk to an adult, the adult would weaken. The same is true regarding ethical sustenance. It must be tailored to children based on their age, and to adults based on their type.

For just as a well-structured and reliable education and guidance must be suited to one's age, so must it be suited to one's type.

Like a garment which must match a person's measure-

---

31. Cf. *Tanchuma, Pekudei,* sec. 3.   32. Blessings recited over foods, etc.

פַּרְשָׁה א בְּסֵדֶר גְדִילָתוֹ שֶׁל אָדָם, בֶּן שָׁנָה דּוֹמֶה לְמֶלֶךְ, בֶּן שְׁתַּיִם וְשָׁלֹשׁ דּוֹמֶה לַחֲזִיר, בֶּן עֶשֶׂר שָׁנָה קוֹפֵץ כַּגְּדִי וְכוּ'.

וְאֵינוֹ דוֹמֶה חִנּוּךְ וְהַדְרָכַת יֶלֶד לְחִינּוּךְ וְהַדְרָכַת נַעַר. חִינּוּךְ הַיֶּלֶד בְּעִקָּרוֹ הוּא בְּעִנְיְנֵי שְׁמִירַת הַנִּקָּיוֹן, צְנִיעוּת וְנִימוּס, שֶׁלֹּא לִהְיוֹת רַעַבְתָן וְכַדּוֹמֶה בְּעִנְיָנִים פְּעוּטִים אֲבָל מוּכְרָחִים, לִהְיוֹתָם יְסוֹד הַהֶבְדֵּל בֵּין מִין הַחַי לְמִין הַמְדַבֵּר. וְחִינּוּךְ וְהַדְרָכַת הַנַּעַר הוּא מְעוּלֶה מִזֶּה וְעִקָּרָם בִּשְׁמִירַת בִּרְכוֹת הַנֶּהֱנִין, לִימוּד, דֶּרֶךְ אֶרֶץ, כִּיבּוּד הוֹרִים, מִשְׁמַעַת לְמוֹרִים. וְאֵינוֹ דוֹמֶה חִנּוּכוֹ וְהַדְרָכָתוֹ שֶׁל נַעַר לְחִנּוּךְ וְהַדְרָכַת הַבָּא לְעוֹנַת בַּר מִצְוָה שֶׁבְּעִיקָרוֹ הוּא בִּשְׁמִירַת קִיּוּם הַמִּצְוֹת בְּהִידּוּר, שְׁמִירַת זְמַנֵּי הַתְּפִלָּה וּבְצִבּוּר, שְׁקִידָה בְּלִימוּד, שְׁמִירַת הַזְּמַן, לְהִתְלַמֵּד מִמִּי שֶׁלְּמַעֲלָה מִמֶּנּוּ, – וְכַךְ הִיא הַמִדָּה בְּחִנּוּךְ וְהַדְרָכָה לְהַעֲלוֹת אֶת הַמְחוּנָךְ וְהַמּוּדְרָךְ מִדַּרְגָּא לְדַרְגָּא עַד אוֹתוֹ הָרוּם הָרָאוּי לוֹ.

וְהַמָּזוֹן הַמּוּסָרִי דּוֹמֶה לְמָזוֹן הַגּוּפָנִי: הַכֹּל יוֹדְעִים כִּי בָּשָׂר טוֹב וּמָרָק חָזָק מְחַזְּקִים כֹּחוֹת הָאָדָם יוֹתֵר מִטִּפַּת חָלָב בְּמַיִם מְתוּקִים, בְּכָל זֶה הִנֵּה אִם יַאֲכִילוּ תִּינוֹק בֶּן חֹדֶשׁ מָרָק חָזָק וּבָשָׂר טוֹב יָמוּת וְאִם יַאֲכִילוּ אֶת הַגָּדוֹל רַק מַיִם מְתוּקִים עִם טִפַּת חָלָב יֶחֱלָשׁ. כֵּן הוּא בְּמָזוֹן הַמּוּסָרִי, אֲשֶׁר צָרִיךְ לְהַתְאִים בַּקְּטַנִּים לְפִי הַגִּיל וּבַגְּדוֹלִים לְפִי הַמִּפְלָגָה.

כִּי כְּשֵׁם שֶׁהַחִנּוּךְ וְהַהַדְרָכָה הַמְסוּדָּרָה וְהַבְּטוּחָה צְרִיכָה לְהַתְאִים אֶל הַגִּיל כֵּן צְרִיכָה לְהַתְאִים גַּם אֶל הַמִּפְלָגָה.

וְכַלְבוּשׁ שֶׁצָּרִיךְ לִהְיוֹת לְפִי מִדַּת הָאָדָם, אִם יְקַצֵּר לֹא

ments—if too short, it is useless, and if too long, a person will stumble—likewise with education or guidanc; if unsuitable, it will not only prove useless, but harmful as well—whether because it fell short of what was required, or whether because it was overly ambitious.

Synopsis

Education and guidance for adults should be geared to their type.[33] For children and youngsters, it should be geared to their age.

9.

A. CLASSIFICATION BASED ON OCCUPATION

People, when classified according to their occupation, fall into one of two categories: full-time Torah scholars, or businessmen.

This division, however, is not indicative of differences in their soul [powers].

On the other hand, a division based on intellectual differences resulting from differences in the manifestation of soul-powers, as explained in Chapter Three,[34] is indeed a division that springs from essential variations of the soul's manifestation. Therefore, a simple fellow cannot usually be transformed into an outstanding intellectual, capable of thinking creatively and grasping profound ideas—if not for some wondrous and highly unusual external cause. Similarly an exceptional sage cannot normally be changed into a common person, unless a punishment—G-d forbid—causes him to fall from his [high] rank—Heaven forefend—since the distinction between a wise person and a plain person is an essential one. The division based on occupation, however, is not an essential one. Thus, a businessman can become a full-

---

33. It is worthwhile to note that the various factors may be combined to produce numerous sub-groupings. For example, the approach needed for

the spiritual-moral education of a rich businessperson who lives in a city will obviously differ from the approach needed for the spiritual-moral educa-

יָבִיא תּוֹעֶלֶת וְאִם יֵאָרַךְ יִכָּשֵׁל בּוֹ, כֵּן הַחִנּוּךְ וְהַהַדְרָכָה
אִם אֵינָם מַתְאִימִים הִנֵּה לֹא זוֹ בִּלְבָד שֶׁלֹּא יָבִיאוּ תּוֹעֶלֶת
אֶלָּא עוֹד יְקַלְקְלוּ בִּשְׁתֵּי הַפָּנִים הֵן אִם יַחְסִיר מֵהַמִּדָּה
הַדְּרוּשָׁה וְהֵן אִם יַגְדִּיל עַל הַמִּדָּה.

קִיצוּר. הִתְחַלְּקוּת הַחִנּוּךְ וְהַהַדְרָכָה בִּגְדוֹלִים לְפִי
הַמִּפְלָגָה וּבִקְטַנִּים וּצְעִירִים לְפִי הַגִּיל.

ט.

א. הַהִתְחַלְּקוּת עַל פִּי עִנְיְנֵי הַהִתְעַסְּקוּת.

הַהִתְחַלְּקוּת עַל פִּי עִנְיְנֵי הַהִתְעַסְּקוּת הַכַּלְכָּלִית שֶׁל
בְּנֵי אָדָם הִיא לִשְׁנֵי סוּגִים כּוֹלְלִים: א) יוֹשְׁבֵי אֹהֶל. ב)
בַּעֲלֵי עֲסָקִים.

הַחֲלוּקָה הַלָּזֹאת אִם כִּי אֵינֶנָּה הִתְחַלְּקוּת נַפְשִׁית

כְּמוֹ שֶׁהוּא הִתְחַלְּקוּת הַמֹּחַ הַבָּאָה מִצַּד הִתְחַלְּקוּת
גִּילוּי כֹּחוֹת הַנֶּפֶשׁ – כַּמְבוֹאָר בְּפֶרֶק ג – שֶׁהִיא הִתְחַלְּקוּת
נַפְשִׁית, וְלָכֵן אָדָם פָּשׁוּט לְעוֹלָם לֹא יֵהָפֵךְ, עַל דֶּרֶךְ
הָרָגִיל בְּטִבְעֵי בְּנֵי אָדָם, לְחָכָם מוּפְלָא בְּהַמְצָאוֹת שְׂכָלִים
וַהֲבָנַת מוּשְׂכָּלוֹת עֲמוּקוֹת, אִם לֹא עַל יְדֵי סִיבָּה מְחוּצָה
לוֹ שֶׁהוּא לְמַעְלָה מִדֶּרֶךְ הָרָגִיל בְּדֶרֶךְ פֶּלֶא, וְכֵן הֶחָכָם
מוּפְלָא לְעוֹלָם לֹא יֵהָפֵךְ לְאִישׁ הֲמוֹנִי, עַל דֶּרֶךְ הָרָגִיל
בְּטִבְעֵי בְּנֵי אָדָם, אִם לֹא מִצַּד הָעֹנֶשׁ חַס וְשָׁלוֹם לִהְיוֹת
נוֹפֵל מִמַּדְרֵיגָתוֹ רַחֲמָנָא לִצְלָן, כִּי הֶחָכָם וְהַהֲמוֹנִי
הִתְחַלְּקוּתָם הִיא הִתְחַלְּקוּת נַפְשִׁית. אֲבָל הַהִתְחַלְּקוּת
הַבָּאָה בְּסִבַּת הַהִתְעַסְּקוּת אֵינָה הִתְחַלְּקוּת נַפְשִׁית, וְלָכֵן

tion of a poor businessperson who
lives in a small town.

34. Possibly the reference is to Pro-

vision Three, the subject of the sixth
chapter, as Chapter Three does not
appear to address this topic.

time Torah scholar, and a full-time Torah scholar can become a businessman.

Nevertheless, as long as they are involved in their respective vocations, whether as a Torah scholar or as a businessman, their situations differ—in that which they need or are compelled to do, and in that which they are compelled to refrain from doing.

It is a readily accepted fact that a full-time Torah scholar belongs to a category superior to that of a businessman, [though] not [superior to that of] a craftsman or laborer.[35] Likewise, it is certainly agreed that people with essentially different natures also act differently in business matters: a wise and talented individual, even while involved in business, is markedly different than ordinary business people. Yet, even a person of refined character is still far removed from the category of a full-time Torah scholar.

In view of the above, basic differences necessarily exist regarding the obligations of the two groups in terms of Torah study and conduct, for these are two very different lifestyles. A full-time Torah scholar: 1) controls his own time, 2) lives a tranquil life, and 3) finds himself only in proper and superlative surroundings. In the case of a businessman, however: 1) his time is not his own—since even when he conducts himself properly [in scheduling his business affairs], he is still deemed, according to the Torah, to be [legitimately] preoccupied [while earning a livelihood]; 2) business, by its very nature, is harrying, and most business people do not live a tranquil life; 3) the nature of his work brings him in contact with various types of people, and occasionally he finds himself in unsavory surroundings.

Therefore, the education and guidance that can be imparted to Torah scholars, as explained by Rabbi Schneur Zal-

---

35. The meaning of this last clause seems unclear. The bracketed text inserted by the translator suggests one possible interpretation. Namely, that the stark contrast between the life of a full-time Torah scholar and the life of a businessman is considerably greater than the contrast between that of the full-time Torah scholar and a working person (who is not a businessperson

הִנֵּה הַבַּעַל עֵסֶק יָכוֹל לְהֵעָשׂוֹת יוֹשֵׁב אֹהֶל וְיוֹשֵׁב אֹהֶל יָכוֹל לְהֵעָשׂוֹת בַּעַל עֵסֶק.

בְּכָל זֶה הִנֵּה בְּעֵת חַיּוּתָם מַה שֶּׁהֵם, אִם יוֹשֵׁב אֹהֶל אוֹ בַּעַל עֵסֶק, הֵם מִתְחַלְּקִים בְּמַצָּבָם בְּמַה שֶּׁצְּרִיכִים אוֹ מֻכְרָחִים לַעֲשׂוֹת וּבְמַה שֶּׁהֵם מֻכְרָחִים לִמְנוֹעַ מִלַּעֲשׂוֹתָם.

דָּבָר מֻחְלָט בְּמוּשְׂכָּל רִאשׁוֹן כִּי סוּג הַיּוֹשְׁבֵי אֹהֶל נַעֲלֶה מִסּוּג הַבַּעֲלֵי עֵסֶק – וְלֹא הַבַּעֲלֵי מְלָאכָה וַעֲבוֹדָה – וְגַם זֶה מוּסְכָּם בְּמוּחְלָט כִּי הֶבְדֵּל מַהוּתִי בְּנֵי אָדָם יֵשׁ לָהֶם יַחַס יָדוּעַ בְּהַשְׁפָּעָה גַּם עַל עִנְיְנֵי הִתְעַסְּקוּתָם, דְּמִי שֶׁהוּא חָכָם וּבַעַל כִּשָּׁרוֹן הִנֵּה גַּם בְּהִתְעַסְּקוּתוֹ בְּמַשָּׂא וּמַתָּן יִהְיֶה מֻבְדָּל מִשְּׁאָרֵי בַּעֲלֵי עֲסָקִים, אֲבָל עִם זֶה הִנֵּה גַּם הוּא – הַבַּעַל צוּרָה מִצַּד מַהוּתוֹ – רָחוֹק עֶרְכּוֹ מִסּוּג הַיּוֹשֵׁב אֹהֶל.

אֲשֶׁר עַל כֵּן הִנֵּה בְּהֶכְרֵחַ אֲשֶׁר הַבַּעֲלֵי עֲסָקִים וְיוֹשְׁבֵי אֹהֶל יִתְחַלְּקוּ בְּמַה שֶּׁהֵם מְחוּיָּבִים בְּלִימוּד וּבְהַנְהָגָה, כִּי הֵם שְׁנֵי דְּרָכִים מְחוּלָקִים זֶה מִזֶּה. הַיּוֹשֵׁב אֹהֶל: א) עִתּוֹתָיו בְּיָדוֹ. ב) חַי חַיֵּי מְנוּחָה. ג) יָכוֹל לְהִמָּצֵא רַק בְּאוֹתָהּ סְבִיבָה הָרְאוּיָה וְהַמְעוּלָה. לֹא כֵן הַבַּעֲלֵי עֲסָקִים א) אֵין עִתּוֹתָם בְּיָדָם, כִּי גַּם הַמִּתְנַהֵג בְּהַנְהָגָה טוֹבָה עַל פִּי תּוֹרָה הוּא עָסוּק. ב) הָעֲסָקִים מַטְרִידִים בְּטִבְעָם, וְרוֹב בַּעֲלֵי עֲסָקִים אֵינָם חַיִּים חַיֵּי מְנוּחָה. ג) מִצַּד עִנְיְנֵי הָעֲסָקִים מִזְדַּמְּנִים הֵמָּה עִם אֲנָשִׁים שׁוֹנִים וְלִפְעָמִים נִמְצָאִים הֵמָּה בִּסְבִיבָה לֹא טוֹבָה.

וְלָזֹאת הִנֵּה אוֹתוֹ הַחִינּוּךְ וְהַהַדְרָכָה שֶׁאֶפְשָׁר לְחַנֵּךְ וּלְהַדְרִיךְ אֶת הַיּוֹשְׁבֵי אֹהֶל כְּמוֹ שֶׁכָּתַב רַבֵּינוּ נִשְׁמָתוֹ עֵדֶן

---

per se). For a regular workingman ("a craftsman or laborer"), like a full-time Torah scholar, may also control his own time, may also live a relatively stress-free life, and may also work in a religiously-friendly environment. In this sense, then, the full-time Torah scholar class is superior to that of the business class, but not superior to that of the working class. See *infra*.

man of Liadi in *Tanya*, chapter 30,[36] cannot be imparted to businesspeople, as it is impossible for a businessman to conduct himself in all his ways as a Torah scholar. In matters permitted by the Torah, there are certainly differences between them. Some actions when performed by businessmen could not be considered transgressions or sins. But for Torah scholars such conduct would be unpardonable, and would be a desecration of G-d's Name.

Synopsis
Education or guidance that is appropriate for full-time Torah scholars is inappropriate for businesspeople.

10.

B. CLASSIFICATION BASED ON FINANCIAL CIRCUMSTANCES: POOR OR RICH

This classification of [people according to] wealth and poverty is based on natural differences, since habit [due to wealth or poverty] profoundly affects the ingrained character of people of both classes, as the saying, "Habit becomes nature."[37]

Wealth and poverty are, by nature, essentially antithetical. A wealthy individual is by nature firm: 1) in his self-confidence, 2) in his self-esteem,[38] and 3) in his expansiveness.[39] 4) He is haughty and arrogant, 5) ridicules the poor, and exalts in their humiliation. A poor person [in contrast] is 1) weak in his self-confidence, 2) contrite, 3) broken, 4) disheartened and 5) self-deprecating.[40]

---

36. Expounding on *Avot* 2:4, "Do not judge your fellow until you come to his place," Rabbi Schneur Zalman writes that "it is [a businessman's] 'place' that causes him to sin, because his livelihood requires him to go to the market for the whole day... where his eyes behold all the temptations.... It is different however, with one who remains in his house for the greater

part of the day...."
Hence, as our text spells out, it is impossible for a businessman to conduct himself in all his ways as a Torah scholar.

37. *Pachad Yitzchak*, s.v. "*hergel*"; *Kitzur Shulchan Aruch*, sec. 32, par. 8; cf. *Yoma* 86a.

בְּסֵפֶר שֶׁל בֵּינוּנִים פֶּרֶק ל' אִי אֶפְשָׁר לְחַנֵּךְ וּלְהַדְרִיךְ אֶת
בַּעֲלֵי הָעֲסָקִים, כִּי הוּא דָּבָר הַנִּמְנָע אֲשֶׁר הַבַּעַל עֵסֶק
יִתְנַהֵג בְּכָל תַּהֲלוּכוֹתָיו כְּמוֹ הַיּוֹשֵׁב אֹהֶל, כִּי בִּדְבָרִים
הַמּוּתָּרִים עַל פִּי תוֹרָה הִנֵּה בְּוַדַּאי יֵשׁ הֶבְדֵּל בֵּין הַבַּעֲלֵי
עֲסָקִים לְיוֹשְׁבֵי אֹהֶל, דְּיֵשׁ דְּבָרִים אֲשֶׁר אֵין עָוֹן וְחֵטְא
לְבַעֲלֵי עֲסָקִים אִם מִתְנַהֲגִים כֵּן, וּדְבָרִים אֵלּוּ עַצְמָם אִם
הַיּוֹשְׁבֵי אֹהֶל מִתְנַהֲגִים כֵּן לְחֵטְא לֹא יְכוּפַּר יֵחָשֵׁב לָהֶם,
וְהֵם בְּכְלַל מְחַלְּלֵי שֵׁם שָׁמַיִם.

קִיצוּר. הַחִנּוּךְ וְהַהַדְרָכָה הָרְאוּיָה לְיוֹשְׁבֵי אֹהֶל אִי
אֶפְשָׁר לְבַעֲלֵי עֲסָקִים.

י.

ב. הַהִתְחַלְּקוּת עַל פִּי הַמַּצָּב הַכַּלְכָּלִי: עֲנִיִּים אוֹ עֲשִׁירִים.

הַחֲלוּקָה הַלָּזֹאת דַּעֲשִׁירוּת וַעֲנִיוּת הִיא חֲלוּקָה
טִבְעִית, לִהְיוֹת הָרְגִילוּת חוֹקֶקֶת בְּכָל אֶחָד מֵהֶם טִבְעוֹ
הַתּוֹלַדְתִּי כְּמַאֲמָר הֶרְגֵּל נַעֲשֶׂה טֶבַע.

הָעֲשִׁירוּת וְהָעֲנִיוּת הֵם, בַּטֶּבַע, הֲפָכִים בְּעֶצֶם מַהוּתָם.
הֶעָשִׁיר הוּא חָזָק: א) בְּהַאֲמָנָתוֹ בְּעַצְמוֹ. ב) בְּהַוָּותוֹ. ג)
בְּרוֹחַב לְבָבוֹ. ד) גֵּאֶה וְגַס רוּחַ. ה) מְבַזֶּה עֲנִיִּים וּמִתְכַּבֵּד
בִּקְלוֹנָם. הֶעָנִי: א) חָלוּשׁ בְּהַאֲמָנָתוֹ בְּעַצְמוֹ. ב) נִדְכֶּה. ג)
נִשְׁבָּר. ד) מְכֻוָּוץ. ה) מַשְׁפִּיל עַצְמוֹ.

---

38. *Behavato*, in the Hebrew. Cf. Psalms 52:9. *Rashi, ad loc*, interprets the word as denoting wickedness. Other commentators suggest "scheming" or "treachery." The translation here, however, follows the interpretation of *Ibn Ezra* there, which in our context seems to fit best.

39. Lit., "expansiveness of heart." Cf.

Proverbs 21:4.

40. Though the rich and poor are *predisposed* to the character traits mentioned above, they do not *necessarily* in fact possess them. There may be mitigating factors, one of which is the case in point, namely, one's education.

Among these ten characteristics of wealth and poverty are the finest of virtues, and [conversely,] the worst of faults. The inferior [traits] among these, whether those of the prosperous or those of the poor, are deplorable; and the fine ones are not always absolutely good. For example, the attribute of self-confidence is a remarkable virtue. Inasmuch as man is human, it is an indispensable quality. Nevertheless, it is not always commendable.

If employed in worthy pursuits—in the study of Torah and the observance of the commandments, or in the process of self-refinement—then self-confidence is a very positive trait and will bring much benefit. It empowers and strengthens an individual, helping him: to study intensively; to ascend from one level to the next in intellectual pursuits; to subdue, to break and to uproot one's bad characteristics; and to develop sterling qualities. A person with self-confidence will not find it daunting to grasp profound concepts or to develop fine characteristics.

The above applies, however, only when this self-confidence is directed towards good and beneficial ends. But if it is used for lowly purposes, as is the nature of the vacuous among the affluent, whose wealth blinds them, then regarding such people the verse says, "Wealth is kept for its owner to his detriment,"[41] for such self-confidence is a breeding ground for human ails.[42]

Similarly, a broken-hearted and self-effacing nature is counted among those noble traits inestimable in value. When used for a good and beneficial purpose, it places a person on the highest pedestal of human virtues. But when springing from poverty and need, it dims the light of one's intelligence and emotions, for then it causes mental sluggishness and emotional lethargy.[43]

---

41. Ecclesiastes 5:12.

42. Lit., "a muddied well for (breed-

ing) human maladies." See Proverbs 25:26, *Rashi, ad loc*; also *Likkutei Dib-burim* (Eng. ed.), vol. 2 pp. 117-119.

בַּעֲשָׂרָה טִבְעֵי הָעֲשִׁירוּת וְהָעֲנִיּוּת הָאֵלּוּ הִנֵּה יֵשׁ בָּהֶם
מֵהַמְּעוּלֶּה בְּמַעֲלוֹת וּמֵהַגָּרוּעַ בְּחֶסְרוֹנוֹת. הַפְּחוּתִים שֶׁבָּהֶם
גְּרוּעִים הֵם בֵּין שֶׁהֵם מִטֶּבַע הָעֲשִׁירוּת וּבֵין שֶׁהֵם מִטֶּבַע
הָעֲנִיּוּת וְהַמְּעוּלִים שֶׁבָּהֶם הֵם גַּם כֵּן מִדָּה וְלֹא מִדָּה.
לְדוּגְמָא: טֶבַע הָאֱמָנַת אָדָם בְּעַצְמוֹ הִיא מַעֲלָה נִפְלָאָה
לִהְיוֹתָהּ מוּכְרַחַת לְהָאָדָם בַּאֲשֶׁר הוּא אָדָם. אֲבָל עִם זֶה
הִנֵּה הִיא מִדָּה וְלֹא מִדָּה.

הָהֶאֱמָנָה בְּעַצְמוֹ אִם בָּאָה לְתַכְלִית מְעוּלָּה, בְּלִימּוּד
הַתּוֹרָה וְקִיּוּם הַמִּצְוֹת וּמִדּוֹת טוֹבוֹת, הִיא מִדָּה טוֹבָה
בִּמְאֹד אֲשֶׁר תָּבִיא תּוֹעֶלֶת מְרוּבָּה. הִיא נוֹתֶנֶת כֹּחַ וָעוֹז
בִּידִיעַת הַלִּמּוּדִים בְּעִיּוּן וְלַעֲלוֹת מִדַּרְגָּא לְדַרְגָּא
בְּמוּשְׂכָּלוֹת, לְהַכְנִיעַ לְשַׁבֵּר וּלְגָרֵשׁ אֶת הַמִּדּוֹת הָרָעוֹת
וּלְהַקְנוֹת בְּעַצְמוֹ אֶת הַמִּדּוֹת הַטּוֹבוֹת, כִּי הַמַּאֲמִין בְּעַצְמוֹ
לֹא יִקְשֶׁה לוֹ מִלְּהַשִּׂיג מוּשְׂכָּלוֹת עֲמוּקוֹת וּמִדּוֹת תְּרוּמִיּוֹת.

אָמְנָם כָּל זֶה הוּא כְּשֶׁמִּשְׁתַּמֵּשׁ עִם טֶבַע הַהֶאֱמָנָה
בְּעַצְמוֹ לְטוֹב וּמוֹעִיל, אֲבָל אִם מִשְׁתַּמֵּשׁ בָּהּ לְתַכְלִית
פְּחוּתָה כְּטֶבַע הָרֵיקָנִין שֶׁבֵּין הָעֲשִׁירִים, אֲשֶׁר הָעֲשִׁירוּת
מְעַוֶּרֶת אוֹתָם, הִנֵּה עֲלֵיהֶם אוֹמֵר הַכָּתוּב עֹשֶׁר שָׁמוּר
לִבְעָלָיו לְרָעָתוֹ וְטֶבַע הַהֶאֱמָנָה בְּעַצְמוֹ הוּא מַעְיָן נִרְפָּשׁ
לְחֶלְאַת בְּנֵי אָדָם.

כֵּן טֶבַע הַלֵּב נִשְׁבָּר וְהַהַשְׁפָּלָה הֵן מִן הַמַּעֲלוֹת הַבִּלְתִּי
מְשׁוֹעָרוֹת בְּרוֹב עֶרְכָּן, לְהַעֲמִיד אֶת הָאָדָם עַל בָּסִיס הֲכִי
נַעֲלֶה בְּמַעֲלַת הָאֱנוֹשִׁיּוּת, כַּאֲשֶׁר מִשְׁתַּמְּשִׁים בָּהֶם לְצוֹרֶךְ
הַטּוֹב וּמוֹעִיל. אֲבָל כַּאֲשֶׁר בָּאִים בְּסִיבַּת הַמַּחְסוֹר מִצַּד
הָעוֹנִי הֵם מוֹרְדֵי אוֹר הַשֵּׂכֶל וְהָרֶגֶשׁ, כִּי גוֹרְמִים טִמְטוּם
הַמֹּחַ וְכִיווּץ הַלֵּב.

---

43. Lit., "constriction of the heart."

Education and guidance must heal ethical sickness and fortify moral well-being. The method of education and guidance appropriate for the nature of the rich, therefore, is different from the method of education and guidance suited to the nature of the poor. And although both require that education and guidance should be structured, the methods themselves, [in the two situations of wealth and poverty,] are different.

Self-confidence is a marvelous quality when used in good and worthwhile endeavors, and is part of a person's natural characteristics insofar as he is human. Yet, it is essentially a negative trait, as the verse says, "Do not rely upon your understanding,"[44] or, in the words of the familiar adage, "He who places his trust in himself is likely to stumble."[45] On the other hand, contriteness and humility, though exalted traits when used in the proper way—as it says, "A contrite and broken heart, G-d, You do not disdain,"[46] and as is written, "For G-d is exalted, He notes the lowly"[47]— are, in and of themselves, negative characteristics. This is so since these traits [of contriteness and humility] are not part of the distinctive qualities of man who is expansive and domineering by nature. Therefore, the task of educating and counselling differs for the wealthy and for the poor according to their respective dispositions.

Synopsis

Ten general characteristics: five associated with wealth and five associated with poverty.

11.

C. CLASSIFICATION BASED ON HABIT, REGARDLESS IF GOOD OR BAD

A habitual trait is one of the most powerful, in and of itself, as well as with regard to its external effects. Although a particular habit is not inborn, it is as forceful as if it were, like

---

44. Proverbs 3:5; *Avot* 4:4.

45. Cf. *Avot* 2:4: "Do not be sure of

yourself until the day you die." The Talmud (*Brachot* 29a) comments, "For Yochanan the High Priest served

הַחִנּוּךְ וְהַהַדְרָכָה צְרִיכִים לְרַפְּאוֹת אֶת חוֹלְאַת
הַמּוּסָרִית וּלְחַזֵּק אֶת הַבְּרִיאוּת הַמּוּסָרִית. לָכֵן אֵינוֹ דּוֹמֶה
אוֹפֶן הַחִנּוּךְ וְהַהַדְרָכָה הַמַּתְאִים לְטֶבַע הָעֲשִׁירוּת לְאוֹפֶן
הַחִנּוּךְ וְהַהַדְרָכָה הַמַּתְאִים לְטֶבַע הָעֲנִיּוּת. וְעִם הֱיוֹת אֲשֶׁר
שְׁנֵיהֶם כְּאֶחָד דּוֹרְשִׁים אֶת תַּפְקִיד הַנְהָגָתָם עַל פִּי חִנּוּךְ
וְהַדְרָכָה מְסֻדֶּרֶת, בְּכָל זֶה הִנֵּה הָאוֹפַנִּים מִתְחַלְּפִים הֵמָּה.

הָאֱמֶנֶת אָדָם בְּעַצְמוֹ אִם הֱיוֹתָהּ מַעֲלָה נִפְלָאָה
לְהִשְׁתַּמֵּשׁ בָּהּ בְּהַטּוֹב וְהַמּוֹעִיל וְהִיא מִטֶּבַע הָאָדָם בַּאֲשֶׁר
הוּא אָדָם, אֲבָל בְּעֶצֶם עִנְיָנָהּ הִיא טֶבַע רָעָה, כְּמַאֲמַר וְאֶל
בִּינָתְךָ אַל תִּשָּׁעֵן, וּכְמַאֲמַר הֶחָכָם הַמַּאֲמִין בְּעַצְמוֹ עָלוּל
לְהִכָּשֵׁל. וְהַלֵּב נִשְׁבָּר וְהַשָּׁפָל אִם הֱיוֹתָן מַעֲלוֹת נִשְׂגָּבוֹת
כְּשֶׁמִּשְׁתַּמֵּשׁ בָּהֶן בְּהַטּוֹב וְהַמּוֹעִיל, כָּאָמוּר לֵב נִשְׁבָּר
וְנִדְכֶּה אֱלֹקִים לֹא תִבְזֶה וּכְתִיב כִּי רָם ה' וְשָׁפָל יִרְאֶה,
אֲבָל בְּעֶצֶם עִנְיָנָם הֵם טְבָעִים רָעִים בְּזֶה שֶׁאֵינָם מִמַּעֲלַת
הָאֱנוֹשִׁיּוּת שֶׁהֵם בַּעֲלֵי רוֹחַב לֵב וְהִשְׁתָּרְרוּת בְּתוֹלַדְתָּם.
וְעַל כֵּן הִנֵּה עֲבוֹדַת הַחִנּוּךְ וְהַהַדְרָכָה מִתְחַלֶּקֶת בִּשְׁנֵיהֶם
כְּפִי עִנְיָנָם.

קִיצוּר. עֲשָׂרָה טְבָעִים כּוֹלְלִים חֲמִשָּׁה בַּעֲשִׁירוּת
וַחֲמִשָּׁה בַּעֲנִיּוּת.

יא.

ג. הַהִתְחַלְּקוּת עַל פִּי הָרְגִילוּת, בְּלִי הֶבְדֵּל אִם טוֹב אִם רָע.

הָרְגִילוּת הִיא אַחַת הַטְּבָעִים הַיּוֹתֵר חֲזָקוֹת בְּעַצְמָן
וְהַיּוֹתֵר חֲזָקוֹת בִּפְעוּלָּתָן עַל מַה שֶׁחוּץ לָהֶן, וְהַיְינוּ עִם
הֱיוֹת שֶׁהָרְגִילוּת בְּאֵיזֶה דָבָר אֵינָהּ עִנְיַן תּוֹלַדְתִּי, עִם זֶה

---

for eighty years, after which he became a Sadducee.

46. Psalms 51:19.

47. Ibid. 138:6.

the saying, "Habit becomes second nature."[37] Aside from its own tremendous innate strength, it is extremely powerful in affecting that which is external to itself; indeed, it affects all [aspects of a person], both the limbs of his body as well as the powers of his soul.

Soul-powers operate in two ways:

1) By influencing at close quarters, as the intellect that influences by explaining and clarifying; be it a matter relating to study or to conduct, the influence of the intellect is pleasant and gentle;

2) By affecting from a distance, by decree, like [the soul-power of] *ratzon,* which influences through rulership and domination.

Habits operate in the second manner, by decree and domination, as the saying, "Over everything, habit reigns supreme."[48] Without any consideration of the matter at hand, be it a minor concern pertaining to the limbs of the body, or be it a major concern pertaining to the soul-powers, habit operates in an autocratic manner, paying no heed to anything outside of itself.

Like the other traits and soul-powers of man, habit serves a most useful role when employed in good and worthwhile endeavors. But when used in worthless and base pursuits, habit becomes utterly terrible. In other words, there are both good and bad habits. It is understood, therefore, that education and guidance, as they pertain to the modification of accustomed behavior, must be structured to suit the nature of the habit. This means that education and guidance must be administered with unswerving resoluteness and with a specific intent: to bolster and enhance good habits, and to destroy and uproot bad ones, so that they are wholly obliterated with no remaining vestige.

Now, even a good habit occasionally requires correction. For example, one who is accustomed to eating good foods

---

48. See *Tishbi,* under the entry for *regel* (habit); cf. *Tanya,* at the end of ch. 14.

הִיא מִדָּה תַּקִּיפָה בְּעַצְמָהּ שֶׁהִיא כְּטִבְעִי מֵהַתּוֹלָדָה, וְכַמַּאֲמָר
הֶרְגֵּל נַעֲשֶׂה טֶבַע שֵׁנִי. וּמִלְּבַד שֶׁהִיא בְּעַצְמָהּ תַּקִּיפָה
בְּיוֹתֵר הִנֵּה הִיא חֲזָקָה בִּמְאֹד לִפְעוֹל גַּם עַל מַה שֶׁחוּצָה לָהּ,
וּפוֹעֵל עַל הַכֹּל בֵּין עַל אֶבְרֵי הַגּוּף וּבֵין עַל כֹּחוֹת הַנֶּפֶשׁ.

שְׁנֵי אוֹפַנִּים הֵם בְּפְעוּלוֹתֵיהֶם שֶׁל כֹּחוֹת הַנֶּפֶשׁ: א)
הַפְּעוּלָה בְּדֶרֶךְ הַשְׁפָּעָה בְּקֵירוּב, כְּמוֹ פְּעוּלַת הַשֵּׂכֶל שֶׁהִיא
הַשְׁפָּעָה בְּדֶרֶךְ קֵירוּב שֶׁמְּבָאֵר וּמַסְבִּיר שֶׁצָּרִיךְ לִהְיוֹת
בְּאוֹפֶן כָּךְ וְכָךְ. בֵּין שֶׁהוּא בְּדָבָר שֶׁל לִימּוּד וּבֵין שֶׁהוּא
בְּדָבָר שֶׁל הַנְהָגָה הִנֵּה הַשְׁפָּעַת הַשֵּׂכֶל בָּא בְּמָתוּן וּבְנוֹעַם.
ב) הַפְּעוּלָה בְּדֶרֶךְ הַשְׁפָּעָה בְּרִיחוּק בִּגְזֵירָה, כְּמוֹ הַשְׁפָּעַת
הָרָצוֹן שֶׁהִיא בְּדֶרֶךְ מֶמְשָׁלָה וּשְׁלִיטָה.

הָרְגִּילוּת פְּעוּלָתָהּ הִיא בָּאוֹפֶן הַשֵּׁנִי, בְּדֶרֶךְ גְּזֵירָה
וּמֶמְשָׁלָה, וְכַמַּאֲמָר הֶרְגֵּל שַׁלְטוֹן עַל כָּל דָּבָר. מִבְּלִי
הִתְחַשֵּׁב עִם הַדָּבָר, אִם הוּא דָּבָר קָטָן מֵהַמִּתְיַחֵס אֶל
אֶבְרֵי הַגּוּף, אוֹ שֶׁהוּא דָּבָר גָּדוֹל הַמִּתְיַחֵס אֶל כֹּחוֹת
הַנֶּפֶשׁ, הִנֵּה בַּכֹּל הָרְגִּילוּת פְּעוּלָתָהּ בְּדֶרֶךְ שְׁלִיטָה מִבְּלִי
הִתְחַשֵּׁב עִם מַה שֶׁחוּצָה לָהּ.

הָרְגִּילוּת הִיא כִּשְׁאָר טִבְעֵי בְּנֵי אָדָם וְכֹחוֹת נַפְשָׁם,
אֲשֶׁר שִׁימּוּשָׁם בְּהַטּוֹב וּמוֹעִיל הוּא יָפֶה מְאֹד וּבְהֶפָּחוֹת
וְגָרוּעַ הוּא רַע מְאֹד, וְהַיְינוּ שֶׁיֵּשׁ רְגִּילוּת טוֹבוֹת וְיֵשׁ
רְגִּילוּת רָעוֹת. אִם כֵּן מוּבָן אֲשֶׁר הַחִינּוּךְ וְהַהַדְרָכָה
בְּהַמִּתְיַחֵס אֶל הָרְגִּילוּת צְרִיכָה לִהְיוֹת מְסוּדֶּרֶת בְּהֶתְאֵם
לְטִבְעֵי הָרְגִּילוּת. וְהוּא שֶׁיִּהְיֶה הַחִינּוּךְ וְהַהַדְרָכָה בְּתוֹקֶף
עֹז בְּאוֹפֶן מְיוּחָד: לְחַזֵּק וּלְפָאֵר אֶת הָרְגִּילוּת הַמְעוּלָּה
וּלְהַאֲבִיד וּלְשָׁרֵשׁ אֶת הָרְגִּילוּת הָרָעוֹת עַד אֲשֶׁר יַכְחִידֵם
וְלֹא יִשָּׁאֵר מֵהֶם אַף גַּם שֵׁמֶץ.

וְגַם רְגִּילוּת הַטּוֹבָה הִנֵּה לִפְעָמִים דּוֹרֶשֶׁת תִּקּוּן, כְּמוֹ
הָרְגִּילוּת בְּמַאֲכָלִים טוֹבִים וּמַעֲדַנִּים בִּשְׁבִיל חִיזּוּק כֹּחוֹתָיו

and delicacies might do so in order to invigorate his faculties, to be able to study assiduously.[49] Although such a practice is well intended, yet this specific habit, in and of itself, leans more towards bad than good. Besides the fact that [a person's interest in] the fine taste of food and drink is degrading to the inherent character of man, it is also contrary to the way of Torah.[50] In this case, education and guidance ought to realign as much as possible the [basically good] habit, to conform to the way of Torah.

Synopsis

Habit, even when regulated, is forceful by nature, acting upon everything by dictate and decree.

12.

D. CLASSIFICATION BASED ON ENVIRONMENT AND PLACE OF RESIDENCE: SMALL TOWN OR LARGE CITY

At first glance, this classification might appear to be a peripheral, a secondary one. In truth, however, this is not so. Locality of residence, whether a small town or a large city, is a primary and fundamental factor affecting the daily conduct of people. The place where a person lives influences every aspect of his life. It affects the person himself: his general attitude,[51] the development of his skills, the expression of his soul-powers, and his conduct. It also affects the lives of one's family members: their education and guidance, and their conduct.

We can deduce the above *a fortiori*. If the life of a man and his family is affected in every respect by the conduct and prevalent attitudes that characterize their wider environment, how much more so is it affected in every respect by the norms and prevalent spirit that characterize the family's immediate community. Moreover, life in a small town is different from life in a large city: life in a small town is more tranquil.

---

49. See *Chavatzelet Hasharon* by R. Moshe Alshich on Daniel 1:5.   50. See *Reshit Chochmah, Shaar Hakedushah* ch. 15; *Mesilat Yesharim* ch. 15.

לִשְׁקוֹד בְּלִימוּד, הִנֵּה כַּוָּנַת הָרְגִילוּת טוֹבָה הִיא אֲבָל גּוּף
וְעֶצֶם הָרְגִילוּת נוֹטֶה יוֹתֵר אֶל הָרַע מֵאֶל הַטּוֹב. וְחוּץ
מִזֶּה אֲשֶׁר מִצַּד מַהוּתוֹ הָעַצְמִי שֶׁל הָאָדָם הִנֵּה מַעֲלַת
טַעֲמֵי הַמַּאֲכָלִים וְהַמַּשְׁקִים פְּחִיתוּת הִיא לְגַבֵּיהּ, הִנֵּה,
מִלְּבַד זֹאת, הֲרֵי זֶה נֶגֶד דַּרְכָּהּ שֶׁל תּוֹרָה, וּבָזֶה צָרִיךְ
לִהְיוֹת הַחִנּוּךְ וְהַהַדְרָכָה לְהַשְׁווֹתָהּ בַּמִּדָּה הָאֶפְשָׁרִית
וְהָרְאוּיָה לְדַרְכָּהּ שֶׁל תּוֹרָה.

קִיצוּר. הָרְגִילוּת גַּם הַמְסוּדֶּרֶת הִיא בְּטֶבַע הַתַּקִּיפוּת,
וּפְעוּלָתָהּ עַל הַכֹּל בְּדֶרֶךְ גְּזֵירָה וְשִׁלְטוֹן.

יב.

**ד. הַהִתְחַלְּקוּת עַל פִּי הַסְּבִיבָה וּמְקוֹם הַמּוֹשָׁב: בְּעִיר
קְטַנָּה אוֹ בְּעִיר גְּדוֹלָה.**

הִתְחַלְּקוּת זוֹ, עִם הֱיוֹתָהּ כַּנִּרְאֶה בְּהַשְׁקָפָה רִאשׁוֹנָה
רַק דָּבָר חִיצוֹנִי וְטָפֵל, בֶּאֱמֶת אֵינָהּ כֵּן, כִּי מְקוֹם הַמּוֹשָׁב
אִם עִיר קְטַנָּה אוֹ גְּדוֹלָה הוּא דָּבָר עִיקָרִי וִיסוֹדִי
בְּאָרְחוֹת חַיֵּי הָאָדָם, כִּי מְקוֹם הַמּוֹשָׁב מַשְׁפִּיעַ, לֹא רַק עַל
כָּל עַנְפֵי הַחַיִּים, בֵּין עַל עַצְמוֹ בְּמַהֲלַךְ רוּחוֹ הִתְפַּתְּחוּת
כִּשְׁרוֹנוֹתָיו וְגִילּוּי כֹּחוֹת נַפְשׁוֹ וְהַנְהָגוֹתָיו, וּבֵין עַל חַיֵּי
הַמִּשְׁפָּחָה חִנּוּכָם וְהַדְרָכָתָם וְהַנְהָגָתָם.

וְהִנֵּה מִלְּבַד זֹאת שֶׁהַדְּבָרִים קַל וָחוֹמֶר: אִם כָּל עַנְפֵי
הַחַיִּים בְּחַיֵּי הָאָדָם וּבְנֵי מִשְׁפַּחְתּוֹ תְּלוּיִים בְּהַנְהָגָתָהּ
וּמַהֲלַךְ רוּחָהּ הַפְּרָטִית שֶׁל אוֹתָהּ הַסְּבִיבָה אֲשֶׁר הוּא
וּבֵיתוֹ נִמְצָאִים בָּהּ, מִכָּל שֶׁכֵּן אֲשֶׁר כָּל עַנְפֵי חַיָּיו וְחַיֵּי
בְּנֵי בֵּיתוֹ תְּלוּיִים בְּהַנְהָגַת וּמַהֲלַךְ רוּחַ הַצִּבּוּר בִּמְקוֹם
מְגוּרוֹ, הִנֵּה עוֹד זֹאת שֶׁהַחַיִּים בְּעִיר קְטַנָּה שׁוֹנִים הֵם, כִּי
הֵם נוֹחִים יוֹתֵר מִבְּעִיר גְּדוֹלָה.

---

51. *Mahalach rucho,* in the Hebrew; lit., "the movement of his spirit."

G-d created man with a unique nature, different not only
from the [nature of] terrestrial and celestial hosts, but also
from the [nature of the] supernal *sefirot.*[52] All these beings possess a single nature, this nature constituting what they are.
Terrestrial creatures have coarse corporeal bodies and are capable of acting [in accordance] with their [one] emotive character in a single way, whether through kindness or mercy, or
severity and cruelty. Celestial hosts have bodies as well,
though their bodies are composed of a subtle substance.
Therefore, they too can act [only] in a single mode, except
that their actions have several beneficial properties. The action of the sun, for example, is to illuminate. Its beneficial
properties are that it heals, improves the growth of vegetation,
ripens fruit and crops, and so on. The supernal creatures—
including both the angels, which are divisible into ten categories, as explained by Maimonides,[53] and the ten *sefirot,*
from *chochmah* to *malchut*—all perform singular actions.
Man, however, is different. He is comprised of both the essential advantages of the supernal [creatures] and the baseness
of the lower [earthly creatures], and his actions are many [and
diverse].[54]

This capacity of man—implanted in him by G-d—to act
in many [diverse] ways is in harmony with both the composi-
tion of his body and the propensities of his soul. Although

---

52. Reality can be divided into four
principal aspects: (1) *Ein Sof*—the Infinite One; (2) *Ohr Ein Sof* (Light of
the Infinite One)—the Self-
manifestation of G-d; (3) the finite
world; and (4) the intermediary levels
in the successive development of the
creative process brought about by
means of the *tzimtzum* (contraction
or reduction).

Of the *Ein Sof,* nothing can be pos-
tulated, except that He is *Ein Sof.*
Names or attributes apply only to
manifestations, to those aspects of Divinity which are revealed in, and to,

His creation. These Divine manifestations or attributes are dimmed radia-
tions from the Light of the *Ein Sof* and
they are called *sefirot.* (*Sefirot*—plural
form; *sefirah*—singular form). The
doctrine of the *sefirot* is first mentioned in *Sefer Yetzirah,* and is briefly
referred to in *Bamidbar Rabbah* 14:12.
The *sefirot* bridge, as it were, the *Ohr
Ein Sof* with the ultimately evolving
world. That is, in order for finite crea-
tions to come about, the Light of the
Ein Sof vested itself in the *sefirot.* Only
by its prior investment in the *sefirot* in
all the intermediary stages brought

הַקָּדוֹשׁ בָּרוּךְ הוּא בָּרָא אֶת הָאָדָם בְּטֶבַע מְיוּחָד
נִבְדָּל מִכָּל הַחַי לֹא רַק בְּצִבְאָ הָאָרֶץ וּצְבָא הַשָּׁמַיִם
אֶלָּא גַּם מֵהַסְּפִירוֹת הָעֶלְיוֹנוֹת. כּוּלָם הֵם בַּעֲלֵי טֶבַע
אַחַת מַה שֶּׁהֵם, דִּצְבָא הָאָרֶץ הֵם בַּעֲלֵי גּוּיָה חוּמְרִית
גַּסָּה וּבַעֲלֵי פּוֹעַל אֶחָד בְּמִדּוֹתֵיהֶם אִם חַסְדָּנִים אוֹ
רַחֲמָנִים אוֹ בַּעֲלֵי גְבוּרָה וְאַכְזָרִים, וּצְבָא הַשָּׁמַיִם עִם
הֱיוֹתָם גַּם כֵּן בַּעֲלֵי גּוּיָה אֲבָל מֵחוֹמֶר הַדַּק, וְגַם הֵם
בַּעַל פּוֹעַל אֶחָד אֶלָּא שֶׁכּוֹלֵל כַּמָּה סְגוּלּוֹת, וּכְמוֹ הַשֶּׁמֶשׁ
שֶׁפְּעוּלָּתוֹ לְהָאִיר, וּסְגוּלָּתוֹ לִרְפָאוֹת, לְהֵטִיב צְמִיחַת
הַדְּשָׁאִים, לְבַשֵּׁל אֶת הַפֵּירוֹת וְהַתְּבוּאוֹת וְעוֹד, וּבְרוּאֵי
מַעְלָה – הֵן הַמַּלְאָכִים הַמִּתְחַלְּקִים לַעֲשָׂרָה סוּגִים כְּמוֹ
שֶׁכָּתַב הָרַמְבַּ"ם וְהֵן הָעֶשֶׂר סְפִירוֹת מֵהַחָכְמָה עַד
הַמַּלְכוּת – הִנֵּה כּוּלָם בַּעֲלֵי פּוֹעַל אֶחָד, נוֹסָף עֲלֵיהֶם
הָאָדָם שֶׁהוּא כָּלוּל מֵהַמַּעֲלָה הָעַצְמִית שֶׁל הָעֶלְיוֹנִים
וּמֵהַפְּחִיתוּת הַגְּרוּעָה שֶׁל הַתַּחְתּוֹנִים וְהוּא בַּעַל פְּעוּלוֹת
רַבּוֹת.

הַפְּעוּלוֹת הָרַבּוֹת שֶׁהִטְבִּיעַ הַקָּדוֹשׁ בָּרוּךְ הוּא בְּהָאָדָם
הִנֵּה הֵם מַתְאִימוֹת לְפִי מֶזֶג גּוּפוֹ וּתְכוּנַת נַפְשׁוֹ. וְהַיְינוּ

---

about by *tzimtzum* could it be vested in a finite and physical world.

The *sefirot* are ten spheres or classes in the following order: *keter* (crown); *chochmah* (wisdom); *binah* (understanding); *chesed* (kindness, grace, benevolence); *gevurah* (might, power, prevalence); *tiferet* (beauty); *netzach* (endurance, victory); *hod* (splendor, majesty); *yesod* (foundation); *malchut* (sovereignty, kingship). In some schemes *keter* is omitted from the order of the ten *sefirot*, and these schemes take *chochmah* as the first of the ten and insert *da'at* (knowledge) as a *sefirah* after *binah*.

53. *Hilchot Yesodei Hatorah 2:7.*

54. Man, by nature, is grafted from numerous different attributes that oppose each other. In the words of Maimonides (*Commentary to Mishnah*, Intro.), "All living creatures and trees have only one function, or two functions...Man, however, can perform many actions that vary from one another." (*Likkutei Torah, Emor* 37c).

terrestrial and celestial creatures possess different types of bodies—the bodies of the former are composed of coarse material, the bodies of the latter are composed of ethereal matter—nevertheless, the actions of both [types of creatures] stem from [and are attributable to] their [respective] bodies. The actions of the supernal *sefirot,* on the other hand, stem from [and are attributable to] their souls. Man, who possesses elements of both the supernal and the non-supernal, acts in a dual manner. Some actions stem from man's body, and others, from his soul.

Among the various traits G-d infused in man is not only the capacity to influence and to affect that which is external to him, but also the susceptibility to be himself influenced and affected by that which is outside of him. For example, man is affected by his food: to refine his understanding and intellect, he must eat refined foods. Similarly, [he should dress with care since donning] fine clothing broadens mental perceptiveness. [Man is likewise influenced by his surroundings. To illustrate:] Those who dwell in small towns enjoy longer life.

Synopsis

Man differs from terrestrial and supernal creatures. His place of residence, either a small or a large city, affects all aspects of his life.

13.

THE FOURTH PREREQUISITE: THE EDUCATOR'S UNDERSTANDING OF THE DESIRABLE AND THE REPUGNANT, AND THEIR LIMITS

There are three fundamental and essential prerequisites in education and guidance regarding a pupil's relationship to his educator or counselor: a) an educator's or counselor's exalted stature in the eyes of his pupil; b) a pupil's trust in his educator or counselor; and c) a pupil's complete compliance and devotion to his educator or counselor.

Also, there are three fundamental and essential pre-

דִּבְרוּאֵי הָאָרֶץ וְהַשָּׁמַיִם, עִם הֱיוֹתָם מַהוּתֵי גוּפִים מְחוּלָּקִים, דְּגוּפוֹת בְּרוּאֵי הָאָרֶץ הֵם חוֹמָרִים וְגוּפוֹת בְּרוּאֵי הַשָּׁמַיִם הֵם גֶּשֶׁם זַךְ, עִם זֶה הִנֵּה שְׁנֵיהֶם פְּעוּלָתָם מִצַּד גוּפָם, וְהַסְּפִירוֹת הָעֶלְיוֹנוֹת הִנֵּה פְּעוּלָתָם הוּא מִצַּד נַפְשָׁם. וְהָאָדָם, שֶׁהוּא כָּלוּל מֵהָעֶלְיוֹנִים וְהַתַּחְתּוֹנִים, הִנֵּה פְּעוּלָתוֹ כְּפוּלָה, הַפְּעוּלָה מִצַּד הַגּוּף וְהַפְּעוּלָה מִצַּד הַנֶּפֶשׁ.

בָּעִנְיָנִים שֶׁהִטְבִּיעַ הַקָּדוֹשׁ בָּרוּךְ הוּא בְּהָאָדָם הִנֵּה, לֹא זוֹ בִּלְבַד שֶׁהָאָדָם הוּא מַשְׁפִּיעַ וּבַעַל פּוֹעַל, אֶלָּא גַם זֹאת שֶׁהָאָדָם הוּא מוּשְׁפָּע וְנִפְעָל גַּם מִמַּה שֶׁחוּצָה לוֹ כְּמוֹ מִמְּזוֹנוֹ, דְּלַזֶּךְ דַּעְתּוֹ וְשִׂכְלוֹ צָרִיךְ לְמַלְאָכִים דַּקִּים וְכֵן בְּעִנְיַן הַבְּגָדִים שֶׁמַּרְחִיבִים דַּעְתּוֹ שֶׁל אָדָם. וְהַיּוֹשְׁבִים בָּעֲיָרוֹת הַקְּטַנּוֹת הִנֵּה יְמֵיהֶם כְּפוּלִים.

קִיצוּר. הָאָדָם מוּבְדָּל מִבְּרוּאֵי מַטָּה וּמַעְלָה, וּמְקוֹם מוֹשָׁבוֹ, עִיר קְטַנָּה אוֹ גְדוֹלָה, מַשְׁפִּיעַ עַל כָּל עַנְפֵי הַחַיִּים.

יג.

תְּנַאי רְבִיעִי: יְדִיעַת הַמְחַנֵּךְ אֶת הַנָּאֶה וְהַמְגוּנֶּה וְהַגְבָּלָתָם.

שְׁלֹשָׁה דְבָרִים יְסוֹדִים וְעִקָּרִים בְּחִנּוּךְ וְהַדְרָכָה – בְּיַחַס הַמְחוּנָּךְ וְהַמּוּדְרָךְ אֶל הַמְחַנֵּךְ וְהַמַּדְרִיךְ: א) רוּם עֶרְכּוֹ שֶׁל הַמְחַנֵּךְ וְהַמַּדְרִיךְ בְּעֵינֵי הַמְחוּנָּךְ וְהַמּוּדְרָךְ. ב) הָאֵמוּן אֲשֶׁר הַמְחוּנָּךְ וְהַמּוּדְרָךְ רוֹחֵשׁ אֶל הַמְחַנֵּךְ וְהַמַּדְרִיךְ. ג) הַמִּשְׁמַעַת בִּמְסִירָה וּנְתִינָה גְמוּרָה שֶׁל הַמְחוּנָּךְ וְהַמּוּדְרָךְ אֶל הַמְחַנֵּךְ וְהַמַּדְרִיךְ.

וּשְׁלֹשָׁה דְבָרִים יְסוֹדִיִּים וְעִקָּרִים בְּחִנּוּךְ וְהַדְרָכָה –

requisites in education and guidance regarding an educator's or counselor's relationship to his pupil: a) close examination of a pupil's essential character, his habits, situation, place of residence, and environment; b) a loving and affectionate rapport between an educator and his pupil; and c) deliberate reflection, from time to time, on a pupil's moral maturation.

An educator or counselor must know full well what is beautiful [i.e. becoming] and what is unbecoming. For what is [defined as] *becoming* is not something absolute, applied identically to all people. Before instructing a pupil, an educator must, therefore, carefully assess each particular matter [separately], and decide whether it is becoming or repulsive [relative to that pupil]. After this deliberation, he should tell his pupil—lovingly and affectionately, with understanding and intelligence, and in a manner of "the words of the wise are heard in quietude"[55]—that this manner of conduct is becoming and should be pursued, and that the other is repulsive and should be shunned.

The more clearly an educator or counselor comprehends what is unbecoming and what is attractive [relative to each pupil], and the more he applies himself to fulfill the aforementioned three provisions in his relationship with his pupil, the more his remarks and directives will be accepted by his pupil. This greater acceptance is attributable not only to his pupil's obedience, but to the pupil's realization that his educator carefully weighs and evaluates beforehand everything [as it relates personally to the pupil]. And although a pupil may not understand the reasoning, his trust in his educator is buttressed, and he will carry out the instructions punctiliously.

Synopsis

Educators and counselors must customize the [definition of] *suitable* and *unsuitable* to each pupil.

---

55. Ecclesiastes 9:17.

א) בְּיַחַס הַמְחַנֵּךְ וְהַמַּדְרִיךְ אֶל הַמְחוּנָּךְ וְהַמּוּדְרָךְ:
הַהִסְתַּכְּלוּת הַחֲזָקָה בְּמַהוּת הַמְחוּנָּךְ וְהַמּוּדְרָךְ בִּרְגִילוּתוֹ
מַצָּבוֹ מְקוֹם מְגוּרוֹ וְהַסְּבִיבָה. ב) יְחוּסֵי אַהֲבָה וְחִיבָּה בֵּין
הַמְחַנֵּךְ וְהַמַּדְרִיךְ וְהַמְחוּנָּךְ וְהַמּוּדְרָךְ. ג) הִתְבּוֹנְנוּת מַתְנָה
שֶׁל הַמְחַנֵּךְ וְהַמַּדְרִיךְ בְּגִידּוּלוֹ הַמּוּסָרִי שֶׁל הַמְחוּנָּךְ
וְהַמּוּדְרָךְ מִזְּמַן לִזְמַן.

הַמְחַנֵּךְ וְהַמַּדְרִיךְ צָרִיךְ לָדַעַת הֵיטֵב אֶת הַנָּאֶה וְאֶת
הַמְגוּנֶּה, כִּי הַנָּאֶה אֵינוֹ עִנְיָן מוּחְלָטִי לְכָל בְּנֵי אָדָם בְּשָׁוֶה,
וְעַל כֵּן צָרִיךְ הַמְחַנֵּךְ וְהַמַּדְרִיךְ לִשְׁפּוֹט הֵיטֵב בְּשִׂכְלוֹ עַל
כָּל דָּבָר וְדָבָר בִּפְרָט אִם הוּא נָאֶה אוֹ מְגוּנֶּה קוֹדֶם
שֶׁיֹּאמַר לְהַמְחוּנָּךְ וְהַמּוּדְרָךְ, וְאַחֲרֵי כֵן יֹאמַר זֹאת
לְהַמְחוּנָּךְ וְהַמּוּדְרָךְ מִתּוֹךְ אַהֲבָה וְחִיבָּה בְּדֵעָה וְהַשְׂכֵּל
בְּדִבְרֵי חֲכָמִים בְּנַחַת נִשְׁמָעִים: דָּבָר זֶה נָאֶה וּצְרִיכִים
לַעֲשׂוֹתוֹ וְדָבָר זֶה מְגוּנֶּה וּצְרִיכִים לְהַרְחִיקוֹ.

כָּל מַה שֶׁהַמְחַנֵּךְ וְהַמַּדְרִיךְ יוֹדֵעַ יוֹתֵר אֶת הַנָּאֶה
וְהַמְגוּנֶּה וְכָל מַה שֶׁהוּא שׁוֹקֵד יוֹתֵר לְמַלֹּאות שְׁלֹשֶׁת
הַתְּנָאִים הָאֲמוּרִים בְּיִחוּסוֹ אֶל הַמְחוּנָּךְ וְהַמּוּדְרָךְ, הִנֵּה
יוֹתֵר וְיוֹתֵר יִתְקַבְּלוּ דְּבָרָיו וְהוֹרָאוֹתָיו אֵצֶל הַמְחוּנָּךְ
וְהַמּוּדְרָךְ. וְלֹא רַק מִצַּד הַמַּשְׁמַעַת שֶׁל הַמְחוּנָּךְ וְהַמּוּדְרָךְ
אֶלָּא מִפְּנֵי שֶׁהַמְחוּנָּךְ וְהַמּוּדְרָךְ רוֹאֶה אֲשֶׁר הַמְחַנֵּךְ
וְהַמַּדְרִיךְ שׁוֹקֵל כָּל דָּבָר וְדָבָר בְּמִשְׁפָּט עִיּוּנִי בֵּינוֹ לְבֵין
עַצְמוֹ, וְאַף גַּם אִם הוּא – הַמְחוּנָּךְ וְהַמּוּדְרָךְ – אֵינוֹ יוֹדֵעַ
טַעֲמוֹ שֶׁל דָּבָר, מִתְחַזֵּק בּוֹ הָאִימוּן בְּהַמְחַנֵּךְ וְהַמַּדְרִיךְ
וִיקַיֵּים אֶת הוֹרָאוֹתָיו בְּדִיּוּק גָּמוּר.

קִיצוּר. הַמְחַנֵּךְ וְהַמַּדְרִיךְ צָרִיךְ לְהַתְאִים אֶת הַנָּאֶה
וְהַמְגוּנֶּה לְפִי הַמְחוּנָּךְ וְהַמּוּדְרָךְ.

14.

THE FIFTH PREREQUISITE: THE EDUCATOR'S DELIBERATE REFLECTION
IN CHOOSING EDUCATIONAL APPROACHES AND METHODS

An educator must review carefully both the virtues and short-comings of a pupil, reflecting on them with great deliberation. With precision, he must assess and weigh each virtue and deficiency in order to neither underestimate nor overestimate them. This is similar to the review and reflection of a craftsman who examines and inspects an item that requires repair.

A craftsman's first step in repairing an article is to disassemble it, taking care not to break even the defective part. Next, he considers every component individually, the flawless as well as the faulty, categorizing each as being good, adequate, or defective. Then, he appraises each part once more, reconsidering whether his classification was accurate. Finally, the craftsman decides the manner of repair: how to remove the faulty piece and with what to replace it, how to improve the adequate parts, and how to reinforce the good pieces. He also reflects on the order of repair, with which part to begin. [Through this systematic approach, he fixes the item properly.] Then [afterwards, when his work is finished], the article leaves his hands in an excellent and beautiful state of repair.

It is unnecessary to explain all the details of this analogy of a craftsman who is diligent in his repair of an article, in its analogue of an educator or counselor who is diligent in his educational work. Indeed, it is impossible to explain all the particulars, except to present some general guidelines, and "give [instruction] to a wise man, and he will become wiser still,"[56] in choosing various forms of education or guidance. Primarily, an educator or counselor must be calm and patient, directing his mind and heart, in a sagacious manner, to even the smallest detail that pertains to a pupil and his education.

---

56. Proverbs 9:9.

יד.

תְּנַאי חֲמִישִׁי: הִתְבּוֹנְנוּת מְתוּנָה שֶׁל הַמַּדְרִיךְ וְהַמְחַנֵּךְ בִּבְחִירַת אוֹפַנֵּי וְדַרְכֵי הַחִינּוּךְ וְהַהַדְרָכָה.

הַמְחַנֵּךְ וְהַמַּדְרִיךְ צָרִיךְ לְהִסְתַּכֵּל הֵיטֵב בְּמַעֲלוֹתָיו וְחֶסְרוֹנוֹתָיו שֶׁל הַמְחוּנָּךְ וְהַמּוּדְרָךְ וּלְהִתְבּוֹנֵן בָּהֶם בִּמְתִינוּת גְּדוֹלָה, לְהַעֲרִיךְ וְלִשְׁקוֹל כָּל מַעֲלָה וְכָל חִסָּרוֹן בַּפֶּלֶס וּמֹאזְנַיִם שֶׁלֹּא לְהַמְעִיט וְלֹא לְהַגְדִּיל, וּכְדוּגְמַת הִסְתַּכְּלוּת וְהִתְבּוֹנְנוּת הָאוּמָּן הַבּוֹדֵק וּבוֹחֵן אֵיזֶה כְּלִי לְתַקְּנָה.

הָאוּמָּן כְּשֶׁהוּא צָרִיךְ לְתַקֵּן כְּלִי הִנֵּה, לְכֹל לְרֹאשׁ, הוּא מְפָרֵק אֶת הַכְּלִי לְאֵבָרָיו בִּזְהִירוּת שֶׁלֹּא לְשַׁבֵּר גַּם אֶת הָאֵבֶר הַמְקוּלְקָל שֶׁבַּהַכְּלִי וְאַחַר שֶׁפֵּרַק אֶת הַכְּלִי לַחֲלָקָיו הֲרֵי הוּא מִתְבּוֹנֵן בְּכָל אֶחָד מֵהֶם, בְּהָרַע כְּמוֹ בְּהַטּוֹב, וּמְחַלְּקָם לְמַעֲרָכוֹת טוֹב בֵּינוֹנִי וָרָע וְאָז וְהִנֵּה עוֹד יוֹסִיף לְהִתְבּוֹנֵן עַל כָּל אֶחָד מִן הַחֲלָקִים אִם הַחֲלוּקָה הַכְּלָלִית לִשְׁלֹשָׁה חֲלָקִים כּוֹלְלִים, טוֹב בֵּינוֹנִי וָרָע, הִיא חֲלוּקָה טוֹבָה. וּבוֹחֵר אוֹפַנֵּי הַתִּקּוּן: אֵיךְ לְהָסִיר אֶת הַמְקוּלְקָל וּבַמֶּה לְמַלֹּאות אֶת מְקוֹמוֹ, אֵיךְ לְתַקֵּן אֶת הַבֵּינוֹנִי לַעֲשׂוֹתוֹ טוֹב, אֵיךְ לְחַזֵּק אֶת הַטּוֹב. וְיִתְבּוֹנֵן בְּסֵדֶר הַתִּקּוּן בַּמֶּה יַתְחִיל תְּחִלָּה וְאָז יֵצֵא הַכְּלִי מִתַּחַת יָדוֹ מְתוּקָן בְּתַכְלִית הַמַּעֲלָה וְהַיּוֹפִי.

לְמוֹתָר לְבָאֵר אֶת כָּל פְּרָטֵי הַמָּשָׁל מֵהָאוּמָּן הַשּׁוֹקֵד בְּתִקּוּן כְּלִי בְּנִמְשָׁל הַמְחַנֵּךְ וְהַמַּדְרִיךְ הַשּׁוֹקֵד בְּחִנּוּךְ וְהַדְרָכָה, אֲשֶׁר אִי אֶפְשָׁר לְבָאֵר כָּל הַפְּרָטִים בַּאֲשֶׁר הֵמָּה כִּי אִם בְּשִׂרְטוּטִים כּוֹלְלִים, וְתֵן לְחָכָם וְיֶחְכַּם עוֹד לִבְחוֹר אוֹפַנֵּי וְדַרְכֵי חִנּוּךְ וְהַדְרָכָה, אֲשֶׁר לְכֹל לְרֹאשׁ צָרִיךְ לִהְיוֹת מָתוּן וְסַבְלָן וְלָשׂוּם דַּעְתּוֹ וְלִבּוֹ עַל כָּל פְּרָט, גַּם הַיּוֹתֵר קָטָן, בְּיַחַס אֶל הַמְחוּנָּךְ וְהַמּוּדְרָךְ וְחִנּוּכוֹ וְהַדְרָכָתוֹ בְּמוֹעֲצוֹת חָכְמָה.

An educator's relationship to his pupil must be very firm and strong. It must be unwavering.

This is so that a pupil will know full well that when given a certain directive about his studies or his conduct, his educator or counselor will not change his mind; nothing will prevent his educator or counselor from ensuring that his instructions are followed—be it through kindness or stern discipline.

Only an extremely resolute and firm education can place a pupil on a truly sound and principled foundation, so that "...even when he grows old, he will not turn from it."[57]

The firmest and most forceful education and guidance, however, must be framed by love and thoughtfulness. Aside from the fact that love and thoughtfulness will make a pupil more receptive to his educator's or mentor's instructions, there are five other benefits to this approach:

1) An educator's stature grows in the eyes of a pupil when he sees the determination of his educator.

2) A pupil sees that the tenacity and resoluteness of his educator or counselor, and his close watch of every detail regarding the pupil's studies or conduct, are motivated not by meanness or anger, but by his love for him.

3) This approach will most assuredly augment:

a pupil's love for his educator,

a pupil's trust in his educator,

a pupil's obedience to his educator, and compliance with his directives.

4) The [firm] conduct demonstrates to a pupil how to apply the attributes of firmness and strength in a worthwhile and beneficial way.

5) This behavior will teach a pupil the fundamentals and principles of decorum and proper behavior.

Synopsis

An educator must relate to his pupil: a) with resolute firmness, and b) in a framework of love and thoughtfulness.

---

57. Ibid. 22:6.

הִתְיַחֲסוּת הַמְחַנֵּךְ וְהַמַּדְרִיךְ אֶל הַמְחוּנָּךְ וְהַמּוּדְרָךְ
צְרִיכָה לִהְיוֹת תַּקִּיפָה וַחֲזָקָה בִּמְאֹד בְּדֶרֶךְ בְּלִי יְשׁוּנֶּה.

בְּאוֹפֶן אֲשֶׁר הַמְחוּנָּךְ וְהַמּוּדְרָךְ יֵדַע בָּרוּר, אֲשֶׁר מְכֵיוָן
שֶׁאָמַר הַמְחַנֵּךְ וְהַמַּדְרִיךְ אֵיזֶה הוֹרָאָה בְּחִנּוּכוֹ וְהַדְרָכָתוֹ,
בְּלִי הֶבְדֵּל אִם בְּלִימוּד אִם בְּהַנְהָגָה, הִנֵּה מִמֶּנָּה לֹא יָשׁוּב
הַמְחַנֵּךְ וְהַמַּדְרִיךְ וְשׁוּם דָּבָר לֹא יְעַכֵּב אֶת הַמְחַנֵּךְ
וְהַמַּדְרִיךְ מִלְּהָבִיא אֶת הַמְחוּנָּךְ וְהַמּוּדְרָךְ – אִם בְּחֶסֶד אִם
בַּשֵּׁבֶט – לָזֶה אֲשֶׁר יְקַיֵּם אֶת דְּבַר הַהוֹרָאָה.

כִּי רַק חִנּוּךְ וְהַדְרָכָה תַּקִּיפָה כְּמְצוּקֵי בַּרְזֶל תּוּכַל
לְהַעֲמִיד עַל בָּסִיס טוֹב וְיָשָׁר בֶּאֱמֶת, אֲשֶׁר גַּם כִּי יַזְקִין
לֹא יָסוּר מִמֶּנָּה.

אָמְנָם הַחִנּוּךְ וְהַהַדְרָכָה הַתַּקִּיפָה וַהֲכִי חֲזָקָה מוּכְרַחַת
לִהְיוֹת בְּמִשְׁבְּצוֹת אַהֲבָה וְנִימוּס מְסוּדָּר. לְבַד זֹאת אֲשֶׁר
הָאַהֲבָה וְהַנִּימוּס מוֹעִילִים לְתוֹעֶלֶת קַבָּלַת הוֹרָאָתוֹ שֶׁל
הַמְחַנֵּךְ וְהַמַּדְרִיךְ בְּחִנּוּכוֹ וְהַדְרָכָתוֹ, הִנֵּה עוֹד זֹאת יֵשׁ בָּזֶה
חָמֵשׁ מַעֲלוֹת: א) מִתְגַּדֵּל עֶרְכּוֹ שֶׁל הַמְחַנֵּךְ וְהַמַּדְרִיךְ בְּעֵינֵי
הַמְחוּנָּךְ וְהַמּוּדְרָךְ, בִּרְאוֹתוֹ תְּקִיפוּת דַּעְתּוֹ שֶׁל הַמְחַנֵּךְ
וְהַמַּדְרִיךְ. ב) הַמְחוּנָּךְ וְהַמּוּדְרָךְ רוֹאֶה, אֲשֶׁר לֹא מִצַּד
הָאַכְזָרִיּוּת אוֹ אֵיזֶה כַּעַס וּקְפֵידָא מִתְנַהֵג עִמּוֹ הַמַּדְרִיךְ
וְהַמְחַנֵּךְ בְּתוֹקֶף גָּדוֹל כָּל כַּךְ וּמְהַדֵּר בְּהַשְׁגָּחָתוֹ עָלָיו עַל כָּל
פְּרָט וּפְרָט, הֵן בְּלִימוּד וְהֵן בְּהַנְהָגָה, כִּי אִם מִצַּד אַהֲבָתוֹ. ג)
בְּהֶכְרֵחַ אֲשֶׁר הַנְהָגָה כָּזוֹ תּוֹסִיף: א) אַהֲבַת הַמְחוּנָּךְ
וְהַמּוּדְרָךְ אֶל הַמְחַנֵּךְ וְהַמַּדְרִיךְ ב) הָאֵמוּן שֶׁל הַמְחוּנָּךְ
וְהַמּוּדְרָךְ בְּהַמְחַנֵּךְ וְהַמַּדְרִיךְ. ג) מִשְׁמַעַת הַמְחוּנָּךְ וְהַמּוּדְרָךְ
אֶל הַמְחַנֵּךְ וְהַמַּדְרִיךְ וְהוֹרָאוֹתָיו. ד) הַנְהָגָה זוֹ מְעוֹרֶרֶת אֶת
הַמְחוּנָּךְ וְהַמּוּדְרָךְ אֵיךְ לְהִשְׁתַּמֵּשׁ בְּמִדַּת הַתּוֹקֶף וְהַחוֹזֶק
בְּהַטּוֹב וּמוֹעִיל. ה) הַנְהָגָה זוֹ תְּלַמֵּד אֶת הַמְחוּנָּךְ וְהַמּוּדְרָךְ
אֶת יְסוֹדֵי וְעִקְּרֵי הַנִּימוּס וְדֶרֶךְ אֶרֶץ.

קִיצוּר. הַנְהָגַת הַמְחַנֵּךְ וְהַמַּדְרִיךְ עִם הַמְחוּנָּךְ וְהַמּוּדְרָךְ
מוּכְרַחַת לִהְיוֹת א) בְּתוֹקֶף עוֹז. ב) בְּמִשְׁבְּצוֹת אַהֲבָה וְנִימוּס.

15.

THE SIXTH PREREQUISITE: PRIORITIZATION IN EDUCATIONAL AP-
PROACHES AND METHODS

Man's essential character is rational. This is the key distinction
between humans and animals, and is what makes man superior.
All of man's deeds, speech and thoughts are in accordance with
his understanding. His emotions as well, to love and to hate; to
extol, to give thanks and to vanquish; to choose the good and
the beautiful, and to despise the bad and the repugnant—are all
dictated by his rational judgment. Nevertheless, [the power of
intellect notwithstanding,] the strength, the power and the
force of man's will control everything [within man].

Man's soul-powers are divided into four groups. These
are: 1) delight [*oneg*] and will [*ratzon*]; 2) wisdom, understanding and knowledge; 3) emotive attributes: love, hate,
pride, gratitude, tenaciousness, etc.; 4) thought, speech and
action. This is in addition to the vital soul that animates the
limbs of the body, enabling them to carry out their respective
functions of providing man with sight, hearing, ambulation,
touch, and so on.

These four groups are [further] divisible into two general
classifications: 1) internal, and 2) encompassing.[58]

The differences between these two classifications are in
four matters:

1) The internal powers are particular, whereas the encompassing powers are general.

2) The internal soul-powers have specific limbs upon and
through which they act, whereas the encompassing powers do
not, for they affect all limbs.[59]

3) Although both are soul-powers, the depth of their re-

---

58. *Makifim,* in the Hebrew. Though
Chasidut makes use of the term
"*makif*" (encompassing) to describe a
certain category of soul-powers, it is
not to be understood in a physical,
spatial sense—that these soul-powers
somehow *surround* the person—

rather, in a figurative sense, as the text
proceeds to describe.

Only the first group of soul-
powers, *oneg* and *ratzon*, are "encompassing." The other three categories are considered "internal."

טו.

תְּנַאי שִׁשִּׁי: הַקְּדִימָה וְאִיחוּר בְּאוֹפַנֵּי וְדַרְכֵי הַחִנּוּךְ וְהַהַדְרָכָה.

הָאָדָם עִם הֱיוֹתוֹ שִׂכְלִי בְּעֶצֶם מַהוּתוֹ, דְּזֶהוּ הַהֶבְדֵּל הָעִקָּרִי בֵּין הַחַי וּבֵין הַמְדַבֵּר וְיִתְרוֹן הָאָדָם עַל הַחַי לִהְיוֹתוֹ שִׂכְלִי וְכָל מַעֲשָׂיו דִּבּוּרָיו וּמַחְשְׁבוֹתָיו הֵם עַל פִּי הַשֵּׂכֶל, וְגַם הַנְהָגַת מִדּוֹתָיו לֶאֱהוֹב וְלִשְׂנוֹא, לְפָאֵר לְהוֹדוֹת וּלְנַצֵּחַ, לִבְחוֹר בְּטוֹב וְנָאֶה וְלִמְאוֹס בָּרַע וּמְגוּנֶּה, הַכֹּל כַּאֲשֶׁר לַכֹּל הוּא עַל פִּי מִשְׁפַּט הַשֵּׂכֶל, עִם זֶה הִנֵּה הָרָצוֹן הֲרֵי כֹּחוֹ גְּבוּרָתוֹ וְתָקְפּוֹ בְּכֹל מָשָׁלָה.

אַרְבַּע חֲלוּקוֹת הֵנָּה בְּכֹחוֹת נֶפֶשׁ הָאָדָם, נוֹסָף עַל נֶפֶשׁ הַחִיּוּנִית הַמְחַיָּה אֶת אֶבְרֵי גוּפוֹ לִפְעוֹל פְּעוּלָתָן בִּרְאִיָּה שְׁמִיעָה הִילוּךְ מִישׁוּשׁ וְהַדּוֹמֶה, וְהֵם: א) עוֹנֶג וְרָצוֹן. ב) חָכְמָה בִּינָה וָדַעַת. ג) מִדּוֹת: אַהֲבָה שִׂנְאָה הִתְפָּאֲרוּת הוֹדָאָה נִצּוּחַ וְהַדּוֹמֶה. ד) מַחֲשָׁבָה דִּבּוּר וּמַעֲשֶׂה.

אַרְבַּע חֲלוּקוֹת הָאֲמוּרוֹת נֶחְלָקוֹת לִשְׁתֵּי מַעֲרָכוֹת כּוֹלְלוֹת א) מַעֲרֶכֶת הַפְּנִימִים. ב) מַעֲרֶכֶת הַמַּקִּיפִים.

שְׁתֵּי הַמַּעֲרָכוֹת הַלָּלוּ חֲלוּקוֹת זוֹ מִזּוֹ בְּאַרְבָּעָה עִנְיָנִים: א) הַפְּנִימִים הֵם כֹּחוֹת פְּרָטִים וְהַמַּקִּיפִים כּוֹלְלִים. ב) הַפְּנִימִים יֵשׁ לָהֶם אֵבָרִים מְיוּחָדִים שֶׁהֵם פּוֹעֲלִים בָּהֶם וְהַמַּקִּיפִים אֵין לָהֶם אֵבָרִים פְּרָטִים לִפְעוֹל בָּהֶם בְּיִחוּד וּפוֹעֲלִים בְּכָל הָאֵבָרִים. ג) הַמַּקִּיפִים וְהַפְּנִימִים, עִם הֱיוֹתָם

---

59. The intellectual attributes—wisdom, understanding and knowledge—are contained within the brain. The emotive attributes are found in the heart. Thought, speech and action, too, have their respective channels within the body. *Oneg* and *ratzon*, in contrast, are not limited to any particular part of the body; there is no specific "limb" of the body through which will or delight are exclusively expressed.

spective roots in the soul itself differs. Encompassing powers are rooted deeper [in the soul].[60]

4) For the most part, the influence and effects of the internal powers come about pleasantly, and from a position of closeness [to what they are influencing and affecting]. The encompassing powers, on the other hand—especially the power of *ratzon*—influence and affect forcefully and dictatorially.[61]

Oneg and *ratzon*, though both encompassing powers, and hence different from the internal powers in the four ways outlined above, are themselves different from one another. It is beyond the scope of this work, however, to elaborate on the soul-powers, their influence and their divisions; only to the extent necessary to sufficiently clarify the subject of education.[62] As such, suffice it to present two general maxims that convey the particular motif of *oneg* and *ratzon:*

1) Nothing [i.e. no soul-power] ranks higher than *oneg.*[63]

2) Nothing is as forceful as *ratzon.* (A variant text: Nothing stands in the way of *ratzon.*[64])

These two succinct sayings express clearly the differences between *oneg* and *ratzon*, notwithstanding their similarity in that they are both encompassing powers. Namely, the main point of *oneg* is its elevation over all, being the initial manifestation of the soul, even though it too is but a faculty of the soul. The outstanding feature of *ratzon* is that it is forceful, and nothing—not a faculty of the soul, or a limb of the body—can oppose it.

---

60. *Oneg* and *ratzon* are rooted within the essence of the soul. Although they are not the essence of the soul itself, but an extension and reflection of it, they are nonetheless the first state of movement from the pure soul toward expression.

61. Since each internal soul-power

has its particular channel of expression within the body, its influence on the person is direct and smooth. *Oneg* and *ratzon*, however, which do not have a particular channel of expression, influence the person in a coercive and forceful manner.

62. See *Translator's Introduction* to

כּוּלָם כְּאֶחָד כֹּחוֹת הַנֶּפֶשׁ, בְּכָל זֶה מִתְחַלְּקִים בְּעוֹמֶק שָׁרְשָׁם בַּנֶּפֶשׁ עַצְמוֹ, שֶׁהַמַּקִּיפִים מוּשְׁרָשִׁים בְּעוֹמֶק יוֹתֵר. ד) הַשְׁפָּעַת הַפְּנִימִים וּפְעוּלָתָם הִנֵּה, בְּמִדָּה יְדוּעָה, הוּא בְּנוֹעַם וּבְקֵירוּב. וְהַמַּקִּיפִים – וּבְעִיקָר הָרָצוֹן – הַשְׁפָּעָתָם וּפְעוּלָתָם הוּא בְּתוֹקֶף וּבְמֶמְשָׁלָה.

הָעוֹנֶג וְהָרָצוֹן, עִם הֱיוֹתָם שְׁנֵיהֶם מִמַּעֲרֶכֶת כֹּחוֹת הַמַּקִּיפִים הַמִּתְחַלְּקִים מִכֹּחוֹת הַפְּנִימִים בְּאַרְבָּעָה עִנְיָנִים הָאֲמוּרִים, עִם זֶה הֲרֵי שְׁנֵי כֹּחוֹת הַלָּלוּ עוֹנֶג וְרָצוֹן גַּם הֵם מִתְחַלְּקִים זֶה מִזֶּה. וּמֵאַחַר שֶׁאֵין הַכַּוָּונָה בְּמַאֲמָר זֶה לְבָאֵר עִנְיְנֵי כֹּחוֹת הַנֶּפֶשׁ הַשְׁפָּעָתָם וְהִתְחַלְקוּתָם בִּפְרָטִיּוּת, כִּי אִם כְּפִי הֶכְרַח הַמְדוּבָּר בָּזֶה, לָכֵן יַסְפִּיק הַקִּיצוּר – בִּשְׁנֵי פִּתְגָּמִים כּוֹלְלִים, שֶׁבָּהֶם מִתְבַּטֵא עִנְיָנָם הַפְּרָטִי דְּעוֹנֶג וְרָצוֹן.

א) אֵין לְךָ דָבָר לְמַעְלָה מֵעוֹנֶג. ב) אֵין לְךָ תַּקִּיף כְּרָצוֹן (נוּסְחָא אַחֲרִינָא: אֵין לְךָ דָבָר הָעוֹמֵד בִּפְנֵי הָרָצוֹן).

שְׁנֵי פִּתְגָּמִים קְצָרִים הַלָּלוּ מַבִּיעִים בָּרוּר אֶת הַהֶבְדֵּל בֵּין הָעוֹנֶג וְהָרָצוֹן בְּעִנְיָנֵיהֶם הַפְּרָטִים נוֹסָף עַל הֱיוֹתָם שְׁנֵיהֶם מַקִּיפִים, וְהוּא – דְּהָעוֹנֶג עִיקָרוֹ שֶׁהוּא לְמַעְלָה מִכֹּל, הַיְינוּ שֶׁהוּא גִילּוּי הָרִאשׁוֹן מֵהַנֶּפֶשׁ עִם הֱיוֹתוֹ גַּם הוּא כֹּחַ הַנֶּפֶשׁ לְבָד, וְהָרָצוֹן הִנֵּה עִיקָרוֹ מַה שֶׁהוּא תַּקִּיף וְאֵין דָּבָר – לֹא בְּכֹחוֹת הַנֶּפֶשׁ וְלֹא בְּאֵבְרֵי הַגוּף – שֶׁיּוּכַל לַעֲמוֹד כְּנֶגְדּוֹ.

On Learning Chasidus (*On the Study of Chasidus*, Kehot 1997, pp. 89 ff).
See also *Likkutei Dibburim* (Eng. ed.), vol. 1. pp. 122-125, where this subject is treated at greater length.

63. *Sefer Yetzirah* 2:7.

64. Cf. *Zohar* II:162b; see also the footnote in *Sefer Hamaamarim 5703*, p. 12.

Synopsis

The powers of the soul are divisible into two classes:

1) internal, and

2) encompassing.

The advantage of *oneg* is in its rank; the advantage of *ratzon* is its forcefulness.

16.

INTRINSIC AND FIGURATIVE ATTRIBUTES

Two adages describing *ratzon* were mentioned above: "Nothing is as forceful as *ratzon*," and "Nothing stands in the way of *ratzon*." They give us detailed insight into the main aspect of *ratzon*, i.e., an appreciation of its broad and forceful influence, both on *oneg*—which is higher than *ratzon*—as well as on the faculties below it. They are all equally affected by *ratzon*, which acts upon them as if by decree and dictate.

All faculties, without exception, can be intrinsic or figurative. This is as equally true of the highest of powers—the power of *oneg*, which because of its pre-eminence is termed a "revelation of the soul"—though it too is still just a power of the soul—as it is true of the lowest of the soul-powers, the power of propulsion,[65] a power possessed also by animals.

The difference between an intrinsic characteristic and a figurative one is that an intrinsic one is all-pervasive, both inwardly and externally, while a figurative term is ascribed—for the sake of comparison—to an external and adjunctive attribute. For example, the cleverness of the fox as likened to the intelligence of man and his understanding. This is the case with regard to *ratzon* as well. Intrinsic-*ratzon* extends into all the powers and limbs in a forceful way, compelling them to act even contrary to their nature. Figurative-*ratzon*, on the other hand, applies only to the simple aspect of wanting, and is influenced by what is out-

---

65. *Zerikah*, in the Hebrew, lit. "throwing."

קִיצוּר. כֹּחוֹת הַנֶּפֶשׁ מִתְחַלְּקִים לִשְׁתֵּי מַעֲרָכוֹת: א) פְּנִימִים ב) מַקִּיפִים, יִתְרוֹן הָעוֹנֶג בְּמַעֲלָה וְהָרָצוֹן בְּתוֹקֶף.

טז.

תּוֹאָרִים עַצְמִים וְתוֹאָרִים מוּשְׁאָלִים.

הַפִּתְגָּמִים הַמְתָאֲרִים אֶת הָרָצוֹן בִּשְׁתֵּי הַנּוּסְחָאוֹת: אֵין לְךָ תַּקִּיף כִּרְצוֹן וְאֵין לְךָ דָּבָר הָעוֹמֵד בִּפְנֵי הָרָצוֹן, נוֹתְנִים לָנוּ מוּשָׂג מְפוֹרָט בְּעִיקַר עִנְיָנוֹ שֶׁל הָרָצוֹן וּמְדִידָה בִּתְקִיפַת הִתְפַּשְּׁטוּתוֹ שֶׁל הָרָצוֹן, הֵן בְּהָעוֹנֶג שֶׁלְּמַעֲלָה מִמֶּנּוּ וְהֵן בְּהַכֹּחוֹת שֶׁלְּמַטָּה מִמֶּנּוּ, לִהְיוֹת כֻּלָּם כְּאֶחָד נִפְעָלִים מִמֶּנּוּ, שֶׁפּוֹעֵל בָּהֶם בְּדֶרֶךְ גְּזֵרָה וּמֶמְשָׁלָה.

וְהִנֵּה בְּכָל הַכֹּחוֹת בְּלִי הֶבְדֵּל, מִן הַכֹּחַ הַיּוֹתֵר עֶלְיוֹן בְּכֹחוֹת הַנֶּפֶשׁ, אֲשֶׁר לְעוֹצֶם גּוֹדֶל הַפְלָאַת מַעֲלָתוֹ, עִם הֱיוֹתוֹ גַּם הוּא כֹחַ הַנֶּפֶשׁ, הִנֵּה הוּא מְתוֹאָר בְּשֵׁם גִּלּוּי הַנֶּפֶשׁ, שֶׁהוּא כֹּחַ הָעוֹנֶג, עַד כֹּחַ הַיּוֹתֵר אַחֲרוֹן בְּכֹחוֹת הַנֶּפֶשׁ שֶׁהוּא כֹּחַ הַזְּרִיקָה – הַשַּׁיָּךְ גַּם בְּבַעַל חַי – יֶשְׁנָם מַה שֶּׁהֵם עַצְמָם וְיֶשְׁנָם שֶׁהֵם בָּאִים רַק בְּהַשְׁאָלָה בִּלְבָד.

הַהֶבְדֵּל בֵּין הָעַצְמִי וְהַמּוּשְׁאָל הוּא, שֶׁהָעַצְמִי הוּא מַה שֶּׁהוּא בְּכָל הֶקֵּיפוֹ, הַיְנוּ פְּנִימִיּוּתוֹ וְחִיצוֹנִיּוּתוֹ. וְהַמּוּשְׁאָל הוּא רַק הַשָּׁוְאָה וְדִמְיוֹן לְאֶחָד מֵעִנְיָנָיו הַחִיצוֹנִים וְהַטְּפֵלִים. לְדוּגְמָא: פְּקִחוּת הַשּׁוֹעֵל לְחָכְמַת הָאָדָם וּתְבוּנָתוֹ. וְכֵן הוּא גַּם בְּעִנְיַן הָרָצוֹן, דְּהָעַצְמִי מִתְפַּשֵּׁט בְּכָל הַכֹּחוֹת וְהָאֵבָרִים בְּתוֹקֶף גָּדוֹל וְאַדִּיר לְהַכְרִיחַ אוֹתָם לַעֲשׂוֹת גַּם מַה שֶּׁהוּא נֶגֶד טִבְעָם, וְהַמּוּשְׁאָל הִנֵּה הוּא רַק מַה שֶּׁהוּא הָרוֹצֶה – א װעהל – וְהוּא מוּשְׁפָּע מִמַּה

side of it, by the dictates of the power of *oneg*, or the power of the intellect. As such, figurative-*ratzon* is the opposite of intrinsic-*ratzon*.

Notwithstanding this fundamental distinction—the intrinsic-*ratzon*'s great inherent forcefulness and strength, and its comparable vigorousness when extending itself, in contrast to figurative-*ratzon* which, in addition to lacking this inherent forcefulness, is [actually] influenced and affected by external stimuli—figurative-*ratzon* also extends itself broadly and most forcefully.

Hence, an educator or counselor must not only proceed slowly with a pupil, as one who teaches an infant to walk, one step at a time, but he must also apply discernment and keen understanding in selecting what to correct first in a pupil. An educator or counselor must be cautious not to attempt to rectify two things at the same time[66]—be it the elimination of a deficiency or the invigoration of a virtue.

For example, if a pupil has two deficiencies: [a)] he exaggerates and lies; b) he is irascible and hot tempered. And in keeping with the nature of all who do not perceive their own blemishes, the pupil's *ratzon* extends with great force into both.

In such a situation, an educator must choose the imperfection to rectify first, giving priority to the more dangerous failing. Given a choice between lying and a hot temper, for example, one should select the hot temper as the shortcoming to focus on initially;[67] for it contains within it the germs of sins and transgressions, such as the wasteful emission of semen, and the like.[68] In turn, these precipitate many maladies, leading to, Heaven forefend, the ruination of body and soul, and mental imbalance, may the Merciful One protect us.

---

66. In other words, since a pupil's *ratzon* is forcefully bent on expressing itself and strongly resists any attempts to restrict it, an educator is well advised to leave an avenue open through which a pupil's *ratzon* can indeed express itself, even if this avenue be a negative behavior of some sort. In this way, the *ratzon*'s resistance to curtailment in the selected critical area is

שֶׁחוּצָה לוֹ, כֹּחַ הָעוֹנֶג אוֹ כֹּחַ הַשֵּׂכֶל, שֶׁזֶּהוּ הֵיפֶךְ מַמָּשׁ מֵהָעַצְמִי דְרָצוֹן.

גַּם הַמּוּשְׁאָל דְּרָצוֹן טִבְעוֹ לְהִתְפַּשֵּׁט, דְּעִם הֱיוֹת שֶׁאֵינוֹ דוֹמֶה כְּלָל לְהָעַצְמִי, דְּהָעַצְמִי, לְבַד זֹאת שֶׁהוּא תַּקִּיף וְחָזָק בִּמְאֹד הִנֵּה תְּקִיפוּתוֹ בְּהִתְפַּשְּׁטוּת גְּדוֹלָה גַּם כֵּן, מַה שֶּׁאֵין כֵּן בְּהַמּוּשְׁאָל שֶׁאֵין בּוֹ תּוֹקֶף הָעַצְמִי וְעוֹד יוֹתֵר שֶׁהוּא מוּשְׁפָּע וְנִפְעָל מְחוּצָה לוֹ, הִנֵּה בְּכָל זֶה הֲרֵי הִתְפַּשְּׁטוּתוֹ הוּא בְּמֶרְחָב וְתוֹקֶף גָּדוֹל.

אֲשֶׁר עַל כֵּן הִנֵּה הַמְחַנֵּךְ וְהַמַּדְרִיךְ, לְבַד זֹאת אֲשֶׁר צָרִיךְ לָלֶכֶת עִם הַמְחוּנָּךְ וְהַמּוּדְרָךְ לְאַט לְאַט, כְּמַרְגִּיל אֶת הַתִּינוֹק לָלֶכֶת צַעַד אַחַר צַעַד, הִנֵּה עוֹד זֹאת צָרִיךְ לְתַקֵּן עִנְיְנֵי הַמְחוּנָּךְ וְהַמּוּדְרָךְ בְּמוֹעֵצוֹת וָדַעַת לִבְחוֹר בַּמֶּה שֶׁצָּרִיךְ לְהַקְדִּים וּלְהִזָּהֵר בְּיוֹתֵר מִלְּהִתְעַסֵּק בְּתִקּוּנֵי שְׁנֵי דְבָרִים, הֵן בַּהֲסָרַת הַחֶסְרוֹנוֹת וְהֵן בְּחִיזּוּק הַמַּעֲלוֹת, בִּזְמַן אֶחָד.

לְדוּגְמָא: אִם הַמְחוּנָּךְ וְהַמּוּדְרָךְ יֵשׁ לוֹ שְׁתֵּי חֶסְרוֹנוֹת: מִגַּם וְשִׁקְרָן: ב) כַּעַסָן וְרַתְחָן, וּכְטֶבַע כָּל אָדָם שֶׁאֵינוֹ רוֹאֶה נִגְעֵי עַצְמוֹ וְדֶרֶךְ אִישׁ יָשָׁר בְּעֵינָיו, רְצוֹנוֹ מִתְפַּשֵּׁט בִּשְׁתֵּיהֶם בְּתוֹקֶף גָּדוֹל.

בְּמָאֹרָע כָּזֶה עַל הַמְחַנֵּךְ וְהַמַּדְרִיךְ לִבְחוֹר בְּאֶחָד מִשְּׁנֵי הַחֶסְרוֹנוֹת לְתַקְּנוֹ תְּחִלָּה. וְיִבְחַר בְּאוֹתוֹ הַחֶסָּרוֹן שֶׁהוּא מְסוּכָּן יוֹתֵר, וּבִשְׁתֵּי הַחֶסְרוֹנוֹת דְּשֶׁקֶר וּרְתִיחָה יִבְחַר הַהִתְעַסְּקוּת תְּחִלָּה בְּחֶסָּרוֹן הָרְתִיחָה, שֶׁיֵּשׁ בָּזֶה חֵטְא וְעָוֹן כְּמוֹ הוֹצָאַת זֶרַע לְבַטָּלָה וְכַדוֹמֶה הַגּוֹרְמִים חֳלָאִים רַבִּים עַד חַס וְשָׁלוֹם אִיבּוּד הַגּוּף וְהַנֶּפֶשׁ שֶׁיּוֹצָא מִדַּעְתּוֹ רַחֲמָנָא לִצְלָן.

---

minimized, and possible rectification of the more serious deficiency facilitated.

67. See *Rambam, Hilchot De'ot* 2:3.

68. See ibid, 3:7.

The educator or counselor who is mindful of the importance of prioritization in behavioral modification methodology—in the reinforcement of virtues and surely in the elimination of deficiencies—possesses a firm basis upon which to anticipate positive results, the achievement of the benefits of educational objectives.

Synopsis

An educator or counselor should involve himself initially in the removal of the (pupil's) most dangerous and repugnant deficiency.

17.

THE SEVENTH PREREQUISITE: PRAISE AND REWARD/REBUKE AND PUNISHMENT IN EDUCATION AND GUIDANCE

G-d implanted in us the nature to delight in praise and to yearn for reward—both moral and material—for upright and proper behavior. He instilled within us the nature to accept rebuke, and to admit the appropriateness of punishment, which misconduct and evil deeds deserve.

As with other inborn or acquired characteristics, this nature is concealed and hidden in the inner recesses of the hearts and minds of pupils. The mandate of educators and counselors is to uncover this nature in their pupils, by fortifying, extolling and polishing their beautiful traits and virtues, and by removing, casting out and uprooting their despicable and coarse characteristics. The receptiveness of a pupil to his education and guidance—and as a result, the success of his education and guidance—are dependent upon an educator's efforts in this regard.

The tools of one's trade are a *sine qua non,* for every artisan, regardless of the type of trade or occupation.[69] This is true of physical, mental, or ethically oriented work—such as teaching, educating or counseling. Only the tools vary with the type of work being performed. The paintbrush in the hand of the artist is like the axe in the hand of the builder. And eth-

---

69. See *Pri Megadim* in his introduction to *Orach Chaim.*

הַמְחַנֵּךְ וְהַמַּדְרִיךְ הַשָּׂם דַּעְתּוֹ וְלִבּוֹ עַל הַסֵּדֶר הַמְסוּדָּר, בִּקְדִימָה וְאִיחוּר בְּאוֹפַנֵּי וְדַרְכֵי הַתִּיקּוּן, בְּהַחְזָקַת וַהֲטָבַת הַמַּעֲלוֹת וּמַה גַּם בִּדְחִיַּית וַהֲסָרַת הַחֶסְרוֹנוֹת, יֵשׁ לוֹ יְסוֹד מוּסָד לְקַוּוֹת לְתוֹצָאוֹת טוֹבוֹת בְּתוֹעֶלֶת הַחִינּוּךְ וְהַהַדְרָכָה.

קִיצּוּר. עַל הַמְחַנֵּךְ וְהַמַּדְרִיךְ לְהִתְעַסֵּק תְּחִלָּה בַּהֲסָרַת הַחִסָּרוֹן הַמְסוּכָּן וּמָאוּס יוֹתֵר.

.יז

תְּנַאי שְׁבִיעִי: הַתִּהְלָה וְהַשָּׂכָר, הַתּוֹכֵחָה וְהָעוֹנֶשׁ בְּחִינּוּךְ וְהַהַדְרָכָה.

הַקָּדוֹשׁ בָּרוּךְ הוּא הִטְבִּיעַ בְּטֶבַע בְּנֵי אָדָם לְהִתְעַנֵּג עַל הַתִּהְלָה וְלִשְׁאוֹף אֶל הַגְּמוּל אֶל בְּשָׂכָר טוֹב – בֵּין מוּסָרֵי וּבֵין גַּשְׁמִי – עַל הַיָּשָׁר וְהַטּוֹב, וּלְקַבֵּל תּוֹכֵחָה וּלְהוֹדוֹת עַל הָעוֹנֶשׁ הַמַּגִּיעַ בְּעַד הָעֲיווֹת וּמַעֲשִׂים רָעִים.

הַטֶּבַע הַלָּזוּ כִּיתֵר הַטְּבָעִים הַבָּאִים מִצַּד הַתּוֹלָדָה אוֹ מִצַּד הָרְגִילוּת, צְפוּנָה וּטְמוּנָה בְּמַעֲמַקֵּי הַלֵּב וְהַמּוֹחַ שֶׁל הַמְחוּנָּכִים וְהַמּוּדְרָכִים וּבַעֲבוֹדַת הַמְחַנֵּךְ וְהַמַּדְרִיךְ לְגַלּוֹתָם – לְחַזֵּק לְפָאֵר וְלִלְטוֹשׁ אֶת הַנָּאוֹתוֹת וְהַמְעוּלּוֹת וְלִדְחוֹת לְהָסִיר וּלְשָׁרֵשׁ אֶת הַמְגוּנּוֹת וְהַפְּחוּתוֹת – תְּלוּיָה קַבָּלַת הַחִינּוּךְ וְהַהַדְרָכָה וְהַהַצְלָחָה בָּזֶה.

הַכְּלָל הַיָּדוּעַ כִּי אֵין אוּמָן בְּלֹא כֵלִים הוּא בְּכָל דְּבַר אוּמָנוּת, בֵּין בַּעֲבוֹדַת מְלָאכָה בֵּין בִּמְלֶאכֶת מַחֲשֶׁבֶת וּבֵין בְּאוּמָנוּת הַמּוּסָרִיּוֹת כְּלִימּוּד, חִינּוּךְ וְהַדְרָכָה, וְאֵין זֶה אֶלָּא מַה שֶּׁכְּלֵי הָאוּמָנוּת מִתְחַלְּפִים לְפִי מַהוּת וְעִנְיְנֵי הָאוּמָנוּת: הַמִּכְחוֹל בִּידֵי הַמְצַיֵּיר הוּא כְּהַגַּרְזֶן בְּיַד הַבַּנַּאי, וּכְלֵי הָאוּמָנוּת הַמּוּסָרִיִּים בִּידֵי הַמּוֹרִים

ical behavioral tools in the hands of teachers, educators and counselors are like the trade tools of artists and builders.

[Extending this analogy,] pupils are like raw material in the hands of educators and counselors. Just as raw material first requires appropriate conditioning, likewise do pupils require proper preparation at the outset, to be receptive to the education and guidance that is suited to them. In this way, they will become upright and goodhearted, besides observing the commandments with a pure faith.

Praise and compliments uplift a pupil, extricating him from his present situation, placing him on a higher plateau. And recompense in the form of a good reward motivates and invigorates a student, animating him with a yearning to ascend from level to level, in both his studies and conduct.

On the other hand, an educator—motivated by a concealed love—must also rebuke a pupil when necessary, pointing a finger at wrongdoings and offenses. This applies whether the misconduct was in a mundane or in a spiritual matter. In either case, an educator ought to discipline him severely for his offense.[70]

An educator or mentor must choose the best and most effective approaches in praising and rebuking, and must select fair and appropriate methods of reward and punishment. That is to say, an educator is obligated to concentrate not only on the measure of praise or rebuke, and on the measure of reward or punishment, but also on the double benefit for a pupil, when the pupil is convinced of his educator's determination and proper conduct. The pupil sees that his educator's admonishments are meted out with propriety and love, punishment is dispensed with purity of heart, and praise and reward are given in an appropriate measure.

Synopsis

In dealing with bad and good [behavior], an educator must be careful when choosing the style of his praise and reproof, and his methods of dispensing reward and punishment.

---

70. See *Chanoch Lanaar, The Ethical Will of Rabbi Shalom DovBer Schneer-* *sohn* (Kehot, 1999), ch. 3.

הַמְחַנְּכִים וְהַמַּדְרִיכִים הֵם כִּכְלֵי הָאוּמָנוּת בִּידֵי הַמְצַיְּירִים וְהַבַּנָּאִים.

הַמְחוּנָּכִים וְהַמּוּדְרָכִים הֵם כַּחוֹמֶר בִּידֵי הַמְחַנְּכִים וְהַמַּדְרִיכִים. כָּל חוֹמֶר דּוֹרֵשׁ הַכְשָׁרָה יְדוּעָה, אֲשֶׁר כֵּן הוּא בְּהַמְחוּנָּכִים וְהַמּוּדְרָכִים, שֶׁצְּרִיכִים לְהַכְשִׁירָם בַּתְּחִלָּה שֶׁיּוּכְלוּ לְקַבֵּל אֶת הַחִינּוּךְ וְהַהַדְרָכָה הָרְאוּיָה לָהֶם, אֲשֶׁר יִהְיוּ יְשָׁרִים וְטוֹבֵי לֵב נוֹסָף עַל שְׁמִירַת קִיּוּם הַמִּצְוֹת בֶּאֱמוּנָה טְהוֹרָה.

הַהִילּוּל וְהַשֶּׁבַח מַגְבִּיהַּ אֶת הַמְחוּנָּךְ וְהַמּוּדְרָךְ, לְהוֹצִיאוֹ מִמַּצָּבוֹ לְהַעֲמִידוֹ עַל בָּסִיס גָּבוֹהַ יוֹתֵר מֵאֲשֶׁר בַּתְּחִלָּה. וְהַגְּמוּל בְּשָׂכָר טוֹב מְעוֹדֵד וּמְחַזֵּק אֶת הַמְחוּנָּךְ וְהַמּוּדְרָךְ לְהָפִיחַ בּוֹ רוּחַ שְׁאִיפַת הָעֲלִיָּה מִדַּרְגָּא לְדַרְגָּא בֵּין בְּלִימוּד וּבֵין בְּהַנְהָגָה.

וּלְעוּמַת זֶה הֵם הַתּוֹכֵחָה – מֵאַהֲבָה מְסוּתֶּרֶת – בְּהוֹרָאָה בָּאֶצְבַּע עַל הָעֲוֹווֹת וְהַחֵטָא – בֵּין בְּמִילֵי דִשְׁמַיָּא וּבֵין בְּמִילֵי דְעָלְמָא – אֲשֶׁר חָטָא הַמְחוּנָּךְ וְהַמּוּדְרָךְ, וּלְעָנְשׁוֹ קָשֶׁה עֲבוּר זֶה.

הַמְחַנֵּךְ וְהַמַּדְרִיךְ צָרִיךְ לִבְחוֹר אֶת הַיּוֹתֵר טוֹב וּמוֹעִיל בְּאוֹפַנֵּי הַשְּׁבָחִים וְהַתּוֹכֵחוֹת וְאֶת הַיָּשָׁר וְנָאוּת בְּדַרְכֵי הַשָּׂכָר וְהָעוֹנֶשׁ. זֹאת אוֹמֶרֶת, אֲשֶׁר הַמְחַנֵּךְ וְהַמַּדְרִיךְ מְחוּיָּיב לָשׂוּם לְבָבוֹ וְדַעְתּוֹ לֹא רַק עַל מְדִידַת הַהִילּוּל וְהַתּוֹכֵחָה וּגְדוֹל הַגְּמוּל בְּשָׂכָר וְעוֹנֶשׁ, כִּי אִם גַּם עַל הַתּוֹעֶלֶת הַכְּפוּלָה שֶׁתַּגִּיעַ לְהַמְחוּנָּךְ וְהַמּוּדְרָךְ אֲשֶׁר יָנֻכַח לָדַעַת תּוֹקֶף דַּעְתּוֹ וְיוֹשֶׁר הַנְהָגָתוֹ שֶׁל הַמְחַנֵּךְ וְהַמַּדְרִיךְ, אֲשֶׁר תּוֹכַחְתּוֹ בְּנִימוּס וּבְאַהֲבָה וְעוֹנְשׁוֹ בְּתֹם לֵב וּמַהֲלָלוֹ וּשְׂכָרוֹ הֵם בְּמִדָּה הָרְאוּיָה.

קִיצוּר. שִׂימַת לֵב הַמְחַנֵּךְ וְהַמַּדְרִיךְ בִּבְחִירַת סִגְנוֹן הַתְּהִלָּה וְהַתּוֹכֵחָה וְאוֹפַנֵּי הַשָּׂכָר וְהָעוֹנֶשׁ לָרָעִים וְלַטּוֹבִים.

APPENDIX

Chasidic Stories

Stories of Rabbi Yosef Yitzchak's Youth

CHASIDIC STORIES

TOLD BY RABBI YOSEF YITZCHAK SCHNEERSOHN
OF LUBAVITCH

DOUBLE STANDARDS

My father, [Rabbi Shalom DovBer Schneersohn of Lubavitch] turned to Rabbi Yehoshua, the *shochet* of Cherson. "Rabbi Yehoshua," he began, "*Bittul* is a crucial and necessary goal, but only when administered to oneself: *self*-abnegation.

"A person should and must engage in self-nullification. Regarding this process, there is an orderly procedure, but others, one should not disparage. Essentially, *bittul* is a push, a shove. Surely, it is a transgression to push a fellow Jew, and if one behaves in such a manner, G-d responds in kind, measure for measure. A famous story is related about this:

"The righteous Rabbi Aaron of Strashele resided in the household of Rabbi Schneur Zalman of Liadi together with the latter's son, Rabbi DovBer. Rabbi Schneur Zalman charged R. DovBer with the responsibility of guiding the younger Chasidim. R. DovBer approached his task by showing love and affection to his young students, even to those whose character traits were lacking. Without exception, everyone was drawn nearer.

"By nature R. Aaron was emotional and passionate. As gifted as he was intellectually, his capacity for feeling was even greater. Sometimes, when the Rebbe taught Torah, R. Aaron had to tie himself with a belt to the table to prevent himself from jumping around in sheer ecstasy.

"There was once a several-month period when R. DovBer was unwell, and R. Aaron assumed his responsibilities. Unlike R. DovBer, R. Aaron was very exacting with the younger Chasidim and chastised them frequently for their faults and failings. Demanding of himself, he applied the same stringent yardstick to his charges.

"R. Aaron later had a private audience with Rabbi

Schneur Zalman, during which he bemoaned a lack of inner vitality in his learning and divine worship. Before responding, Rabbi Schneur Zalman rested his holy head on his arms, and went into a state of *deveikut* (spiritual rapture). Finally, lifting his head, he quoted: 'For according to the work of man shall He pay back to him.'[1] The ways of G-d are measure for measure. If one reproaches a fellow Jew, even if such rebuke is intended for the sake of Heaven, G-d responds in kind—by locking the doors and closing the portals. But when one draws a fellow Jew closer, the gates of Torah and of divine service are thrown open.'"

There are many elements in *avodah* (spiritual service) that must be applied only to the self. And *bittul* (self-abnegation) is one of them. When dealing with others, one must always tread carefully.

The proper path consists of strengthening and encouraging others, drawing them closer with love and affection.

—*Rabbi Yosef Yitzchak's Igrot Kodesh*, vol. 4, pp. 302-3

UNDER THE SPELL OF MUSIC

My great-grandfather, Rabbi Menachem Mendel of Lubavitch, the *Tzemach Tzedek*, was an incredible genius in the revealed dimension of Torah, and in Kabbalah and Chasidus. Besides, he was a genius in geometry. His children and grandchildren, on the other hand, were brilliant in both the revealed dimension of Torah and in Chasidus, yet not one of them inherited his aptitude for geometry. And of his many great-grandchildren, only one was endowed with this faculty.

In the summer of 5655 (1895), my father [Rabbi Shalom DovBer] and I were staying in a summer residence not far from Lubavitch. One day, as we were taking a walk, my father told me the following.

---

1. Job 34:11.

Years before, on Tuesday, 26 Tevet 5637 (11 January 1877), he had asked his own father, Rabbi Shmuel, several questions about the chasidic discourse he had delivered the previous Shabbat.

The conversation then turned to the difference between a *chush* (sense, aptitude) and a *kisharon* (talent, ability). Talents, my grandfather explained, are passed on from parents to children, and may persist for two or three generations. By contrast, a *chush* often resurfaces only in later generations. To illustrate, he related the following anecdote:

In Shevat 5616 (January 1856), the *Tzemach Tzedek* sent his son Rabbi Shmuel and the famed chasid R. Levi Yitzchak—Rabbi Shmuel's brother-in-law—on a mission to Petersburg that would last over two months. Staying at the same hotel on Vansenka Street, in the room adjoining theirs, was an Italian violin virtuoso.

"My brother-in-law," Rabbi Shmuel related, "had an uncommonly keen ear for music. But neither his father, (my uncle Yekutiel, Rabbi DovBer's son-in-law) nor his grandfather, R. Yosef Bunim (Rabbi Levi Yitzchak Berditchever's son-in-law) could sing. But it was this Levi Yitzchak, the fourth generation removed from the *tzaddik* Rabbi Levi Yitzchak of Berditchev, who inherited his ancestor's aptitude for music.

"The Berditchever Rav (as Rabbi Levi Yitzchak of Berditchev was also known), was an exceptional vocalist," Rabbi Shmuel told my father. "Your uncle's *chush* for violin was a lot stronger than for singing.

"One evening," Rabbi Shmuel continued, "I walked into our hotel room and saw your uncle sitting in an armchair with his hands clasped, his eyes wide and glazed, his mouth open. He trembled, as though feverish.

"At first I was alarmed at what I saw. Then, from next door, I heard the strains of a violin, being played by our neighbor, the virtuoso. I realized then that your uncle, given his deep appreciation for music, had fallen under the violin's spell. He was completely captivated by the music."

This same R. Levi Yitzchak is the great-grandfather of the *wunderkind* Yehudi Menuhin,[2] who is a fifth generation descendent of (my great-uncle) Rabbi Levi Yitzchak.

—*Rabbi Yosef Yitzchak's Igrot Kodesh*, vol. 4, p. 381

INTROSPECTION

A chasid who came to speak to [my grandfather] Rabbi Shmuel of Lubavitch at a private audience once lamented the fact that he was devious in every matter that came his way. Rabbi Shmuel thereupon advised him to undertake 600 fasts.

Seeing that he was left astonished, Rabbi Shmuel added: "Do you think that fasting means not eating from sunrise to sunset?! That is called dieting! Fasting is an *avodah*. Spend fifteen minutes every day thinking about yourself earnestly. Guard your tongue from talking. We're not speaking about meditating on Chasidus; we're speaking of simply thinking about yourself." And within two years this chasid had undergone a complete change.

When my revered father, the Rebbe [R. Shalom DovBer], told me of this he added: "He changed not only the faculties of his soul: he changed *in essence*. If you had seen him, that change would have overwhelmed you."

The Talmud often uses the phrase, "That is to say..." In the above story, then, one can find oneself a lesson: everyone should spend fifteen minutes, every day, thinking about himself.

—*Likkutei Dibburim (Eng. ed.), vol. 4, p. 136*

---

2. Famous violinist and conductor (b. April 22, 1916, New York, USA, d. March 12, 1999, Berlin, Germany).

OUR STUDENTS—OUR TEACHERS

Among the fulltime, married students in the *beit midrash* of [my grandfather] Rabbi Shmuel of Lubavitch there was a young chasid who was quite knowledgeable. Though he was not an outstanding scholar, he was at home in the world of scholarship. He was thoroughly familiar with *Likkutei Torah* and the Chasidic works of the *Tzemach Tzedek*, and used to study the Chasidic discourses of Rabbi Shmuel.

When the time came for him to leave the halls of learning for the business world, he entered the study of Rabbi Shmuel and asked, "With what does one leave?"

"Make this your guiding rule," replied Rabbi Shmuel. "Whenever you observe failings in others, know that they exist within yourself. Whenever you observe positive qualities in others, implant them within yourself."

As the Baal Shem Tov teaches, Divine Providence means that if G-d arranges that one should encounter a particular person at a particular time, there is a reason for it. Everyone should thus be a teacher from whom one can learn something. One who does not believe in this principle is a nonbeliever, G-d forbid.

When this young man visited Lubavitch in later years (—I knew him), he said that the advice of Rabbi Shmuel saved him: it set him on his feet. And when he visited the resting place of Rabbi Shmuel, he kissed the soil.

This principle of learning from others should be known by the mentors who guide their people in their divine service, and who may thereby be called *mezakei harabim*, those who make the public meritorious. If they do not know this principle, then (G-d forbid) the opposite may be the case.

—*Likkutei Dibburim (Eng. ed.), vol. 4, pp. 136-138*

STORIES OF RABBI YOSEF YITZCHAK'S YOUTH

TO SAY MODEH ANI

When I was a small child, just beginning to speak, my father said to me: "Every question you have, you should ask me."

When I was taught to recite the *Modeh Ani*, I was instructed to place one hand against the other and bow my head, and say *Modeh Ani* in this position.

When I grew a bit older, I asked my father: "Why, when we say *Modeh Ani*, must we place one hand against the other and bow our head?"

Father replied: "In truth, you should not be asking 'why.' But I did tell you to ask me all your questions." He then sent for the servant Reb Yosef Mordechai, a Jew of eighty years, and asked him: "How do you recite *Modeh Ani* in the morning?"

"I place one hand against the other and bow my head," answered Reb Yosef Mordechai.

"Why do you do so?" asked my father.

"I don't know. When I was a small child, that's what I was taught."

"You see," said Father to me. "He does it so because his father taught him so. And so on back until Moshe Rabbeinu, and until Avraham Avinu who was the first Jew. One should do without asking 'why.'"

"I'm just a little boy," I said in my defense.

"We're all 'little,'" Father replied. "And when we get older, we first begin to understand that we're little."

—*Sefer Hasichot 5709, p. 330*

A CHASIDIC KISS

R. Yosef Yitzchak related: "In the year 5644 [1884—he would have been 3 or 4 years old at the time], our living quarters consisted of two rooms. One room was the bedroom. In the other room, my father would sit and study with his study partner, the chasid Rabbi Yaakov Mordechai Bezpalov. In that room also stood my small bed.

"In those years, I was a beautiful child with a shining face. One night, R. Yaakov Mordechai looked at me in my sleep and remarked to my father that the features and radiance of my face bespoke an inner purity of mind.

"My father was roused with a desire to kiss me. But at that moment there arose in his mind the thought that in the Holy Temple, in addition to the *korbanot*, they would also bring gold, silver, etc. for the upkeep of the Temple. He decided to transform the kiss into a *maamar*. He then wrote the *maamar* beginning *Ma Rabbu Maatecha*.

"In 5652 [1892] my father gave me the manuscript as a gift and said, 'This is a Chasidic kiss; in time I will explain.' In 5656 [1896] he told me the whole story."

—*Likkutei Sichot, vol. 1, p. 138*

TWO EYES

When R. Yosef Yitzchak was four years old, he asked his father: "Why did G-d make people with *two* eyes? Why not with one eye, just as they have one nose and one mouth?"

"Do you know the *Alef-Bet?*" asked his father.

"Yes."

"Then you know that there are two very similar Hebrew letters, the *Shin* and the *Sin*. Can you tell the difference between them?"

"The *Shin* has a dot on its right side, the *Sin* on its left," Yosef Yitzchak replied.

Said his father: "There are things which one must look upon with a right eye, with affection and empathy, and there are things to be regarded with a left eye, with indifference and detachment. On a *Siddur* or on a Jew, one should look with a right eye; on a candy or toy, one should look with a left eye."

—*Sefer Hasichot 5691, pp. 158*

FOLLOWING THE LEADER TO MATAN TORAH

On the eve of Shavuot 5645 [1885], our teacher in *cheder* told us:

"In the Torah it says, 'Moshe brought the nation out toward G-d.' The Jewish people were led by Moshe Rabbeinu to *Matan Torah*, the giving of the Torah.

"Children," our teacher addressed us, "I would like to lead *you* to *Matan Torah!*"

Our teacher led us all—around 30 or 35 pupils—to Reb Binyamin's *Beit Hamidrash*. He said that the next day, the first day of Shavuot, we should get up an hour earlier than usual and meet there in the *Beit Hamidrash* to receive the Torah.

The next day, I awoke at 7 o'clock in the morning, and prepared to proceed to the *Beit Hamidrash*. Since I was an only child, however, my mother held me particularly dear, so she wanted me to taste something before I left. I answered, though, that before *Matan Torah* I didn't want to eat. And so off I walked to the *Beit Hamidrash*. All the pupils gathered there, and afterwards our teacher led us through Chachloyker Street....

* * *

In the past, *chinuch* was something altogether different. Everything was done with *temimut,* simplicity. This was true for the children and for the parents; it was visible both in the pupils and in the parents.

In the past, one had *derech eretz,* respect, for Torah teachers. Nowadays, people say of them, "What do they teach? Old-fashioned things."

In the past, one could feel the simplicity!

On the verse, "*Tamim* you shall be before G-d your

L-rd," R. DovBer of Lubavitch offers his well known interpretation: Through your *temimut*, you can attain [a connection with] the *temimut* of G-d, and the *temimut* of G-d is the simplicity of His Essence.

—Sefer Hasichot 5705, p. 100

FOLLOWING FATHER'S ORDERS

Once, when R. Yosef Yitzchak was about six years old, his father asked him to recite the blessing over his *tzitzit*. He replied that he had already said the blessing earlier that day. "All the same," responded his father. Yosef Yitzchak refused to comply. His father slapped him gently (this was the *only* occasion that his father ever hit him), and said, "When I tell you to do something, you must listen." Unable to restrain himself, Yosef Yitzchak cried, "If the blessing is for the sake of G-d, then I have already said the blessing. But if a blessing is required on account of your instruction, then..."

His father explained, "Indeed, one recites the blessing since G-d has so commanded. Nevertheless, every father is responsible for his children, and as such, his directives must be followed."

—Likkutei Sichot, vol. 2, p. 504-5

WHOLEHEARTED KINDNESS

One day when R. Yosef Yitzchak was a child of seven, he was given a watermelon by his grandmother, the widow of R. Shmuel of Lubavitch. He gave a piece to a little friend, but as soon as they had sat down together on a bench in the courtyard to eat, they were suddenly disturbed by a voice. It was the Rebbe, R. Shalom DovBer, calling his son inside.

When he went in, his father said: "It is true that you gave part of your watermelon to your friend—but you did not give it wholeheartedly."

The Rebbe went on to explain the various levels that may

be attained on the attribute of kindness, as well as the nature of the opposite attribute, and the child wept in remorse to the point that he even felt unwell.

The boy's mother, seeing what had transpired, asked her husband: "What do you want from the child?"

"Everything is in order," the Rebbe reassured her. "This way he will have acquired a positive character trait."

R. Yosef Yitzchak repeated this incident when he had already grown to be Rebbe himself, and concluded with the words: "*That* is education!"

—Sefer Hasichot 5705, pp. 10-11

THE EMBARRASSING SHINY BOOTS

In honor of Pesach 5650 [1890], I received new clothes and new boots. The custom in Lubavitch was that after the *chametz* had been burnt the morning of Pesach eve, we would go off to immerse in the *mikveh*, and then, dressed in our best festive clothes, we would bake the *matzah* that was to be eaten at the *Seder* that evening. Afterwards we would proceed to the other preparations that had to be made for the evening. One of my tasks was to remove the seals from the wine bottles, especially those on which letters were imprinted, and to ease out the stoppers, being careful not to let the corkscrew touch the wine inside.

I did this job in my father's study, and, as he watched my painstaking care not to soil my new clothes in any way—especially my anxiety lest my new boots lose their shine—he said: "Among the commentaries that R. Schneur Zalman of Liadi wrote on the prayers in his edition of the Siddur we find a parable: A nobleman sits at the head of his sumptuous table laden with all manner of choice delicacies. His dog is busy under the table, gnawing bones. Could one picture this aristocrat leaving his table and chair, and crawling under the table, gnawing bones?"

This parable spoke to me so eloquently that I was ashamed to look at my new clothes. *That* is education!

—*Sefer Hasichot 5703, pp. 74-75*

AN ATTITUDE FOR FATHER

...I then remembered how, as a small child, still studying with the late Reb Yekutiel the *melamed,* I would run to the synagogue to listen to Father pray, and how heavy my heart was: Why doesn't Father pray briskly, as the entire congregation does, as my uncles do? I once asked my uncle, Rabbi Zalman Aaron. He told me that Father cannot pronounce the Hebrew words easily. I agonized greatly over this.

Once, I came to the synagogue. Not a soul was to be found, only Father was standing, his face to the wall, praying. He was entreating G-d, pleading for mercy. But I did not understand: Why was he entreating more than all other worshippers? Why did he need G-d's mercy more than other people?

Suddenly, Father began to sob. My heart sank within me: Father was crying! Not a soul in the house of G-d, and Father was crying. I bent an ear and I heard him say, "*Shema Yisrael...,*" and he sobbed, "*Hashem Elokenu...,*" and he sobbed. He then fell silent. And then again, in a powerful voice emerging from the depths of his heart, "*Hashem echad!*" in a flood of tears and a terrifying voice.

This time I could no longer contain myself. I went to my mother (may she live long) and wept: "Why does Father pray longer than all the worshipers? My uncle, R. Zalman Aaron, says that Father has difficulty pronouncing the words. Why can Father not recite Hebrew in a proper speed? And today I saw that Father is crying. Come with me, my mother, I will show you that Father is crying...!"

"What can I do?" responded my mother. "Can I have him sent to *cheder*? Go to your grandmother and ask her, perhaps she can do something about this."

I rushed to take the advice of my mother and went to my late grandmother, the saintly Rebbetzin [Rivkah], and posed to her my innocent question. My grandmother said to me: "Your father is a great *chasid* and *tzaddik*. With each and every word he utters, he first thinks of the meaning of the word that he is saying."

I remember how at that moment she calmed me, and how from then on my attitude towards my father changed; for I then knew that Father is apart from and above other men. With his every move I saw that Father is *Father*. Father awakens in the morning and dons the *tefillin* and reads the *Shema*. Then, he goes to serve his mother tea. (I also wish to do so, but they prevent me by saying that I will be hurt by the boiling water.)

Father washes his hands before meals not like other people. Other people pour water over their hands only twice, but Father takes the pitcher with his right hand, then hands it over to his left hand, and pours three times in succession over his right hand; then he takes another pitcher of water, and, using the towel to hold it in his right hand, pours three times over his left.

Every day, before the afternoon Minchah prayers, Father again goes to serve a cup of tea to his mother and sits there for about an hour.

Everyone speaks, speaking with gusto, but Father is mostly silent. Sometimes he speaks, speaking softly…

—*Likkutei Dibburim vol. 4, pp. 1346-8*

RESPECT FOR A LEAF

It was the summer of 5656 [1896], and Father and I were strolling in the fields of Balivka, a hamlet near Lubavitch. The grain was near to ripening, and the wheat and grass swayed gently in the breeze.

Said Father to me: "See G-dliness! Every movement of each stalk and grass was included in G-d's Primordial

Thought of Creation, in G-d's all-embracing vision of history, and is guided by Divine providence toward a G-dly purpose."

Walking, we entered the forest. Engrossed in what I had heard, excited by the softness and seriousness of Father's words, I absentmindedly tore a leaf off a passing tree. Holding it a while in my hands, I continued my thoughtful walking, occasionally tearing small pieces of leaf and casting them to the winds.

"The Holy Ari[1]," Father said to me, "says that not only is every leaf on a tree a creation invested with Divine life, created for a specific purpose within G-d's intent in creation, but also that within each and every leaf there is a spark of a soul that has descended to earth to find its correction and fulfillment.

"The Talmud," Father continued, "rules that, 'A man is always responsible for his actions, whether awake or asleep.'[2] The difference between wakefulness and sleep is in the inner faculties of man—his intellect and emotions. The external faculties function equally well in sleep, only the inner faculties are confused. So dreams present us with contradictory truths. A waking man sees the real world, a sleeping man does not. This is the deeper significance of wakefulness and sleep: when one is awake one sees Divinity; when asleep, one does not.

"Nevertheless, our sages maintain that man is always responsible for his actions, whether awake or asleep. Only this moment we have spoken of Divine Providence, and, unthinkingly, you tore off a leaf, played with it in your hands, twisting, squashing and tearing it to pieces, throwing it in all directions.

"How can one be so callous toward a creation of G-d? This leaf was created by the Almighty towards a specific purpose and is imbued with a Divine life-force. It has a body and it has its life. In what way is the 'I' of this leaf inferior to yours?"

—Likkutei Dibburim vol. 1, pp. 168-70

---

1. Acrostic for Rabbi Yitzchak Luria (1534–1572); universally accepted father of modern kabbalistic thought. 2. *Bava Kama,* 26a.

OTHER TITLES IN
THE CHASIDIC HERITAGE SERIES

THE ETERNAL BOND *from Torah Or* $9.00

By Rabbi Schneur Zalman of Liadi
Translated by Rabbi Ari Sollish

This discourse explores the spiritual significance of *brit milah*, analyzing two dimensions in which our connection with G-d may be realized. For in truth, there are two forms of spiritual circumcision: Initially, man must "circumcise his heart," freeing himself to the best of his ability from his negative, physical drives; ultimately, though, it is G-d who truly liberates man from his material attachment.

ৰ্ভ ৰ্ভ ৰ্ভ

JOURNEY OF THE SOUL from *Torah Or* $12.00

By Rabbi Schneur Zalman of Liadi
Translated by Rabbi Ari Sollish

Drawing upon the parallel between Queen Esther's impassioned plea to King Ahasuerus for salvation and the soul's entreaty to G-d for help in its spiritual struggle, this discourse examines the root of the soul's exile, and the dynamics by which it lifts itself from the grip of materiality and ultimately finds a voice with which to express its G-dly yearnings. Includes a brief biography of the author.

ৰ্ভ ৰ্ভ ৰ্ভ

FLAMES from *Gates of Radiance* $14.00

By Rabbi DovBer of Lubavitch
Translated by Dr. Naftoli Loewenthal

This discourse focuses on the multiple images of the lamp, the oil, the wick and the different hues of the flame in order to express profound guidance in the divine service of every individual. Although *Flames* is a Chanukah discourse, at the same time, it presents concepts that are of perennial significance. Includes the first English biography of the author ever published.

ৰ্ভ ৰ্ভ ৰ্ভ

THE MITZVAH TO LOVE YOUR
FELLOW AS YOURSELF from *Derech Mitzvotecha* $9.00

By Rabbi Menachem Mendel of Lubavitch, the Tzemach Tzedek
Translated by Rabbis Nissan Mangel and Zalman Posner

The discourse discusses the Kabbalistic principle of the "collective soul of the world of *Tikkun*" and explores the essential unity of all souls. The discourse develops the idea that when we connect on a soul level, we can love our fellow as we love ourselves; for in truth, we are all one soul. Includes a brief biography of the author.

తా తా తా

TRUE EXISTENCE *Mi Chamocha 5629* $12.00

By Rabbi Shmuel of Lubavitch
Translated by Rabbis Yosef Marcus and Avraham D. Vaisfiche

This discourse revolutionizes the age-old notion of Monotheism, i.e., that there is no other god besides Him. Culling from Talmudic and Midrashic sources, the discourse makes the case that not only is there no other god besides Him, there is nothing besides Him—literally. The only thing that truly exists is G-d. Includes a brief biography of the author.

తా తా తా

TRUE EXISTENCE *The Chasidic View of Reality* $14.00

A Video-CD with Rabbi Manis Friedman

Venture beyond science and Kabbalah and discover the world of Chasidism. This Video-CD takes the viewer step-by-step through the basic chasidic and kabbalistic view of creation and existence. In clear, lucid language, Rabbi Manis Friedman deciphers these esoteric concepts and demonstrates their modern-day applications.

తా తా తా

YOM TOV SHEL ROSH HASHANAH 5659
Discourse One $11.00
By Rabbi Shalom DovBer of Lubavitch
Translated by Rabbis Yosef Marcus and Moshe Miller

The discourse explores the attribute of *malchut* and the power of speech while introducing some of the basic concepts of Chasidism and Kabbalah in a relatively easy to follow format. Despite its title and date of inception, the discourse is germane throughout the year. Includes a brief biography of the author.

෴෴෴

FORCES IN CREATION
Yom Tov Shel Rosh Hashanah 5659 Discourse Two $10.00
By Rabbi Shalom DovBer of Lubavitch
Translated by Rabbis Moshe Miller and Shmuel Marcus

This is a fascinating journey beyond the terrestrial, into the myriad spiritual realms that shape our existence. In this discourse, Rabbi Shalom DovBer systematically traces the origins of earth, Torah and souls, drawing the reader higher and higher into the mystical, cosmic dimensions that lie beyond the here and now, and granting a deeper awareness of who we are at our core.

෴෴෴

THE FOUR WORLDS $11.00
By Rabbi Yosef Yitzchak of Lubavitch
Translated by Rabbis Yosef Marcus and Avraham D. Vaisfiche
Overview by Rabbi Immanuel Schochet

At the core of our identity is the desire to be one with our source, and to know the spiritual realities that give our physical life the transcendental importance of the Torah's imperatives. In this letter to a yearning Chasid the Rebbe explains the mystical worlds of Atzilut, Beriah, Yetzira, and Asiya.

ᵴᵴᵴ

GARMENTS OF THE SOUL
Vayishlach Yehoshua 5736 $7.00
By Rabbi Menachem M. Schneerson, the Lubavitcher Rebbe
Translated by Rabbi Yosef Marcus
Often what is perceived in this world as secondary is in reality most sublime. What appears to be mundane and inconsequential is often most sacred and crucial. Thus at their source, the garments of the human, both physical and spiritual, transcend the individual.

ᵴᵴᵴ

THE UNBREAKABLE SOUL
Mayim Rabbim 5738 $7.00
By Rabbi Menachem M. Schneerson, the Lubavitcher Rebbe
Translated by Rabbi Ari Sollish
The discourse begins with an unequivocal declaration: No matter how much one may be inundated with materialism, the flame of the soul burns forever. This discourse speaks to one who finds pleasure in the material world, yet struggles to find spirituality in his or her life.

ᵴᵴᵴ

ON THE ESSENCE OF CHASIDUS
Kunteres Inyana Shel Toras Hachasidus $12.00
By Rabbi Menachem M. Schneerson, the Lubavitcher Rebbe
In this landmark discourse, the Lubavitcher Rebbe, Rabbi Menachem M. Schneerson, explores the contribution of Chasidus to a far deeper and expanded understanding of Torah. The Rebbe analyzes the relationship Chasidus has with Kabbalah, the various dimensions of the soul, the concept of Moshiach and the Divine attributes—all in this slim volume.

ᵴᵴᵴ

COMING SOON!

YOM TOV SHEL ROSH HASHANAH 5659
Discourse Three
By Rabbi Shalom DovBer of Lubavitch
Translated by Rabbi Y. Eliezer Danzinger

HACHODESH 5700
By Rabbi Yosef Yitzchak of Lubavitch
Translated by Rabbi Yosef Marcus